THE ULTIMATE HOCKEY DRILL BOOK

VOLUME 2

RICHARD TRIMBLE

MASTERS PRESS

A Division of Howard W. Sams & Co.

Published by Masters Press
A Division of Howard W. Sams & Company
2647 Waterfront Pkwy E. Dr, Suite 100, Indianapolis, IN 46214

Printed in the United States of America.

97 98 99 00 01 02   10 9 8 7 6 5 4 3 2 1

Trimble, Richard M.
       The ultimate hockey drill book / Richard M. Trimble.
           p.   cm.
       Contents: v. 2.
       ISBN 1-57028-143-2 (v. 2 : pbk.)
       1. Hockey--Coaching.   I. Title.
       GV848.25.T75 1997   97-20413
       796.962'2--dc21   CIP

   Participation in the game of ice hockey is by its very nature dangerous, so drills need to be properly supervised, taught and demonstrated. Coaches must always be cognizant of potential hazards, including flying pucks, hard checks and the ability levels of players relevant to the difficulty of drills being called for. Neither the author nor the publisher of this book accept responsibility for any injuries incurred during the execution of any drill described herein.

CONTENTS

To Dad, Dick Trimble

INTRODUCTION

It hints of an oxymoron to suggest that the Ultimate Hockey Drill Book (singular) should appear in two volumes. While my original vision was for a single book containing about 250 drills, my final compilation of drills exceeded 450 and that is when my editor at Masters Press wisely suggested that we divide the work into two volumes for the sake of manageability. It was a good call.

I was thrilled when I saw the first volume in print, but my thoughts went immediately to the second volume because I was excited about what I knew was in it. Contained in this follow-up work are some of the more creative drills such as off-ice training and goalie drills, positional drills both individualized and team oriented, transition drills and advanced combination skills drills.

As I suggested in the first volume, drills are the products of imagination born of the necessity of instruction and this second volume reflects that. Taken together, I am very pleased with both books as I feel that they represent a "complete package." The response to volume one has been deeply gratifying and I hope that both books are as helpful to you in your coaching as the drills have been to me in mine.

Coach Richard "Rick" Trimble
September, 1997

A PHILOSOPHY OF DRILLS

Every drill must have a specific intent. As obvious as that seems, it is often overlooked. The coach must ask himself what he hopes to impart to his players through the drill about to be executed. Is the intention skill enhancement, instruction, agility, or conditioning? Having discerned this, considerations then range into the duration of the drill, timing of the drill in practice, amount of ice surface needed, and equipment to be used. The tempo of the drill should be considered, too.

For instance, if the drill is purely instructional, then it falls into a low-tempo mode and it may only be employed once. An agility drill should not last longer than five to seven seconds in duration or it falls into the conditioning category. A conditioning drill should be high tempo and most often should be placed at the end of practice. On a cautionary note, conditioning drills should always relate to specific skills utilized in the sport that you teach. Why on earth, for example, do hockey coaches insist on punishing recalcitrant players with on-ice pushups? Suicide sprints, board jumps and the like are more grueling and they impart not only the message but a hockey-specific skill, too. Skill enhancement drills can be repetitive and part of a regular practice routine. Furthermore, the tempo will vary in accordance with the age and skill level of the players you are working with. The more advanced they are, the more you can insist on a higher tempo.

This book will be broken down into the aforementioned drill orientations: instructional, agility, skill enhancement and conditioning. It is the coach's responsibility to create his drills with a specific philosophy in mind.

It is my firm belief that about 75 percent of what is drilled on the ice can be taught off the ice. Moreover, off-ice drills can definitely be used to enhance, not just impart, on-ice skills.

As a further thought, when designing your drill sequence and practice plan, why not separate drills with drills? In other words, rather than waste precious ice-time by setting up cones and so forth while the players stand around, have them loop the rink in a designated free-skating drill while you are performing your set-up/clean-up chores. Use one such drill per practice and then have the players move on the whistle. It shows organization and it sets an atmosphere of a good work ethic and team hustle. Plus, you have maximized ice-time usage.

When you are "installing" drills, or teaching them for the first time, it can be helpful to use only half of the ice (if the drill allows this) to see that the players get it before working a mirrored replica of the drill to the other side or coming back the other way.

To keep your drills flowing despite misplayed passes or overskated pucks, place a coach with a collection of pucks at a strategically located position on the ice (endzone or neutral zone) to feed players on a drill pattern who have lost their puck.

In short, keep things moving!

PRACTICE ORGANIZATTON

What drill book would be complete without a few thoughts on how best to integrate and utilize the drills explained? It is truly surprising how many coaches do not know how to effectively organize and orchestrate a practice session. With ice hockey being one of the few sports in which the practice time is often a costly affair financially, coaches must come to practice prepared with a definite drill sequence and practice plan.

Conceptually, the coach should break his or her practice time into four components: warm-up, individual skills, combined skills or team work, and conditioning. In the beginning of the season, more work will probably be spent honing individual skills in preparation for the season. As the team runs through the regular game season, then combination work and team work may assume a greater percentage of the practice time. The coach will need to work on things that the team is not doing well or executing to satisfaction. All four components of the practice session will always be present however; the difference lies in what is to be emphasized.

Combination drills such as passing 3-on-0 or 2-on-2 are helpful in the early and preseason as the coach will be looking for effective and workable tandems, lines and player pairings.

During the season, one of the strongest pieces of advice I can offer is also one of the simplest: take notes. I coach both baseball and ice hockey and throughout my career of over 25 years I have always made a notepad as necessary to my coaching attire as my habitual chewing gum. In the heat of a game, you will never remember all of the corrections you need to make, things you want to say and changes you may wish to think about. Write them down. These game notes, often dictated to the team statistician on the bench, will help you compose your practice plan for the next time your team works out. I find that I must even jot down a word to two on the things that I want to mention to my team in between periods or innings. Some coaches save these notes game-to-game and even year-after-year, but I generally discard them after I have made the necessary adjustments and corrections.

Another aspect of the "write it down" philosophy relates to the practice plan itself. Frame out what you want to work on and then commit it to writing. Run copies so that all of your coaches are literally on the same page. This is advice that is as sound for the college coach as it is for the clinic coach. By writing out the plan, you will be able to keep to the time frame allocated. Hockey coaches cannot waste precious ice-time for the financial reasons stated earlier.

Warm-ups and conditioning must be related to the sport. In ice hockey, your pre-practice warm-ups involve skating and stretching rather than static and stationary stretches, although the latter does have its place off the ice. The conditioning phase, always scheduled for the end of practice, must also relate directly to the game of hockey. Sprints with start-and-stop cross-overs, board jumps, positional windsprints and so forth must enhance not only the athlete's physical stamina, but also his or her sport-specific skills.

Think it out, write down, and then teach and drill. Keep your practices focused, efficient and on time. Bring a dry-mark "blackboard" with you so that drills can be diagrammed prior to their execution. Photocopy pages from this book and write in your own time of duration and coaching points, as shown on each page.

It's all here. Now it's up to you to make things work.

KEY

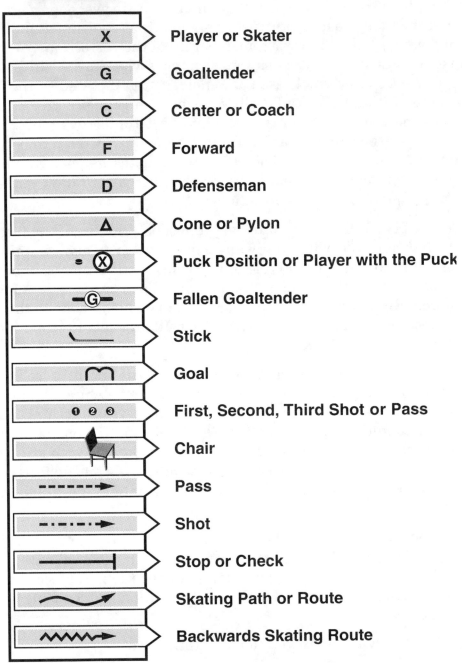

X	Player or Skater
G	Goaltender
C	Center or Coach
F	Forward
D	Defenseman
△	Cone or Pylon
⊗	Puck Position or Player with the Puck
—G—	Fallen Goaltender
⌐	Stick
⌒	Goal
❶ ❷ ❸	First, Second, Third Shot or Pass
	Chair
------▶	Pass
—·—·—▶	Shot
——⊤	Stop or Check
～⤳	Skating Path or Route
ᴧᴧᴧᴧ▶	Backwards Skating Route

Note that the drills are basically set up in each chapter in an order of difficulty with the easier drills in the beginning of each chapter and proceeding to more difficult ones at the end.

HI–TEMPO AND ADVANCED PASSING AND SHOOTING DRILLS

— Cycling
— Transition
-- Team Play

"The will to excel and the will to win, they endure. They are more important than any events which occasion them."

— Vince Lombardi

NAME OF DRILL: Transition Breakout Drill
SKILL TO BE TAUGHT/ENHANCED: Defenseman/Wing Coordination

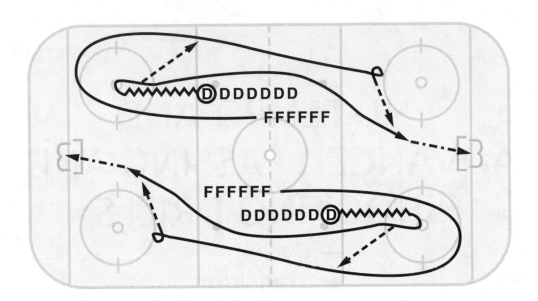

DESCRIPTION OF DRILL:

- Work both sides of the ice simultaneously in this drill. Align your defensemen and forwards in their respective lines as shown. Defensemen have the pucks.
- On the whistle, the defensemen will backskate with the puck to base of the faceoff circle. The forward curls around him or her, as shown, and breaks up ice to receive the breakout pass from the defenseman.
- The forward will attack the far goal as a 1-on-0 or they can use the defenseman, who has joined the rush as a trailer, 2-on-0.
- When switching sides to replicate the drill to the other side, be sure to send players across the ice rather than diagonally down the ice.

COACHING POINTS:

- An element that this drill enhances is that of hitting the moving winger with the outlet or breakout pass. All too often wingers will sit along the boards waiting for the breakout pass instead of reading transition and moving forward for the pass.
- Both will rush up ice 2-on-0, but obviously the forward will arrive ahead of the defenseman. Have them do a "turn-up," as shown and pass off to the defenseman breaking in.

NAME OF DRILL: Hi-Speed Board Passing Drill
SKILL TO BE TAUGHT/ENHANCED: Board Passing on the Fly

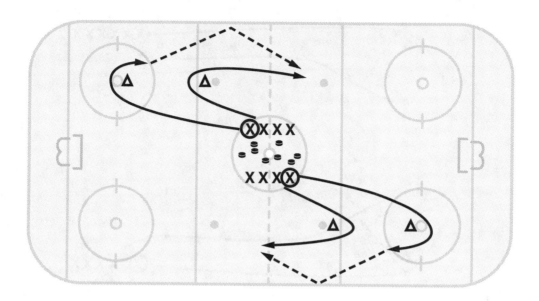

DESCRIPTION OF DRILL:
- Players align at center-ice as shown.
- On the whistle, the first two players will break for their designated cones, the lead player having a puck.
- Once the lead player reaches the lower cone, he passes off the boards to the second player who carries in for a shot.
- As soon as the deeper, passing player releases the pass, the next player in line carries a puck to the deeper cone to repeat the drill. Only this time he will pass to the former lead player in line.

NAME OF DRILL: Angle-Back Passing Drill
SKILL TO BE TAUGHT/ENHANCED: Tactical Pass

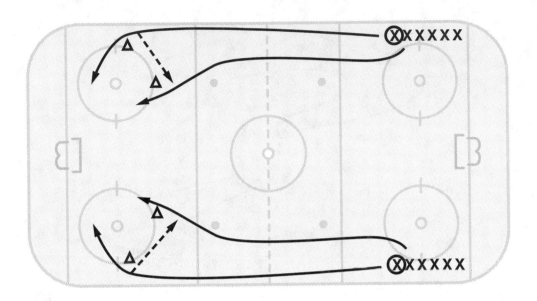

DESCRIPTION OF DRILL:
- For advanced players and teams, the back diagonal pass is an out-standing tactical pass, but it must be learned and read. That is the purpose of this drill.
- Set lines of players along the boards at one end of the ice.
- The lead player carries the puck to the far cone; he/she then drops the puck back to the trailing player who was second on line and broke 2-3 seconds later than his partner did.
- Use the cones to read placement.
- The drop passer should also read the stick-side of the person he/she is passing to.

COACHING POINTS:
- Divide the offensive zone into "thirds." Set cones at the top third, middle third and bottom third to vary the reads.
- Note that this is not a true drop pass per se, but rather a pass which is dropped back to a trailing player; it is offset to the side rather than directly backward.

NAME OF DRILL: Lake State Drill
SKILL TO BE TAUGHT/ENHANCED: Passing, Support, Breakouts

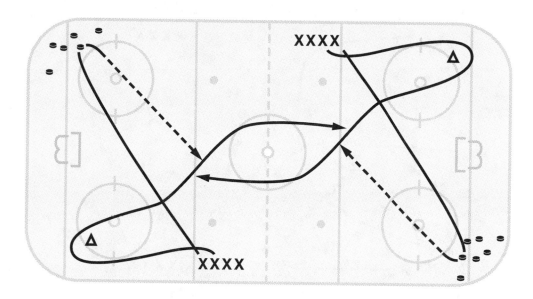

DESCRIPTION OF DRILL:
- Align the players just outside the blue lines in the neutral zone as shown.
- On the whistle two players will break simultaneously. The front man will break into the far corner to pick up a loose puck while the second man in line curls around the cone as shown.
- The corner man will outlet pass to the second man who will carry in for a shot while the passer joins the other line across the ice.

COACHING POINTS:
As the players tire, the supporting gap distance will increase; keep reminding them and strive for a 15' distance between the passer and receiver.

NAME OF DRILL: Garden State Passing Drill
SKILL TO BE TAUGHT/ENHANCED: Passing and Shooting

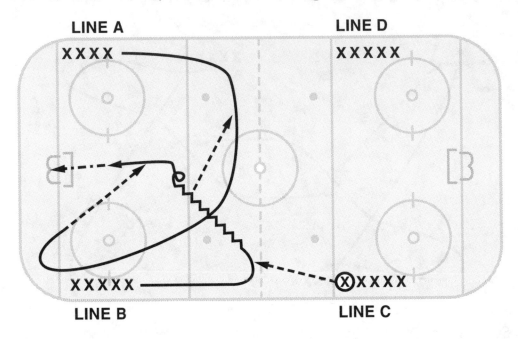

DESCRIPTION OF DRILL:
- This drill (so named because I took it from the tryouts for the presti-gious Garden State Games in New Jersey) involves a multiplicity of passing skills.
- Line A will begin without a puck but will eventually receive one from a player in Line B who is working his/her way through their own course. The pass recipient from Line A will carry into the offensive corner and pass out to the waiting player in Line B who should position himself in the high slot area for a shot on goal.
- Line B will also begin without a puck but will receive one from a player in Line C. He/she will receive this pass as they are skating toward the Line C players; they then pivot into a backskate mode and it is in this mode they will hit the circling player from Line A with the pass that they will eventually receive for a shot on goal.

COACHING POINTS:
Replicate this drill at the other end of the ice with a Line C and D.

NAME OF DRILL: 3-0 to 2-1 Transition Drill
SKILL TO BE TAUGHT/ENHANCED: Offensive and Defensive Patterns
and Skills

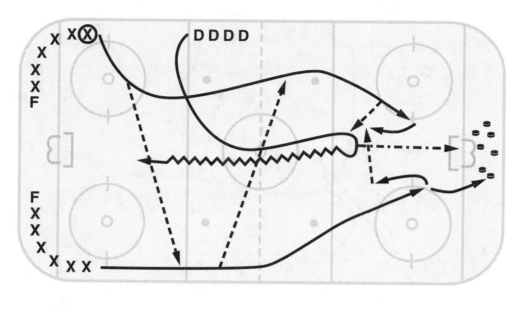

DESCRIPTION OF DRILL:
- Line the forwards in the corners and the defensemen in the neutral
  zone as shown.
- On the whistle, the two forwards will break up ice on a 2-on-0 only to
  be joined by a trailing defenseman once they reach the neutral zone.
  Have the attackers work the puck to the pointman for a shot while the
  forwards skate for the net, "crashing" it, as they say.
- After the shot is taken, either the rebound or a loose puck picked up
  behind the net is retrieved for a return break up ice as a 2-on-1 against
  the defenseman.

NAME OF DRILL: More 3-0/2-1 Transition
SKILL TO BE TAUGHT/ENHANCED: Passing, 2-1 Play, Transition

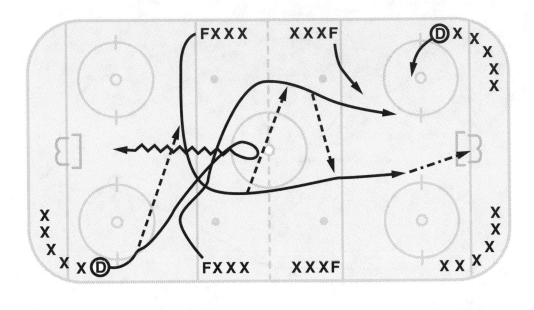

DESCRIPTION OF DRILL:
- Align defensemen in corners and forwards in the neutral zone as shown. Defensemen have the pucks.
- Beginning at one end of the ice, the defenseman will outlet to one of the two forwards cycling in the neutral zone along the blue line. They will then attack 3-0 but the defenseman will trail only to the red line.
- That defenseman will then pick up the two forwards attacking from the other end and play them, 2-on-1, in a defensive mode.

NAME OF DRILL: Full Zone Passing Drill
SKILL TO BE TAUGHT/ENHANCED: Passing and Shooting

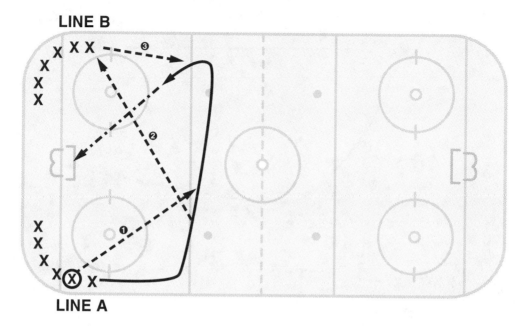

DESCRIPTION OF DRILL:
- This drill will involve three passes and a shot on goal.
- On the whistle, the lead player in Line A will break for the blue line, receive a pass from the second player in Line A, pass across the ice to the lead player in Line B and continue skating the blue line until reaching the far point as shown.
- The skating player will take in a pass from Line B and execute any of three shots on goal: slapshot, walk-in and shoot, or shot-off-the-pass.*
- Alternate sides, as once the player in Line B passes, he/she must break the opposite way.

COACHING POINTS
*This shot is NOT a one-timed shot, but rather one that is taken when the player draws the pass in and with one sweeping motion, drives it on goal.

NAME OF DRILL: Full-Ice Three-Pass Drill
SKILL TO BE TAUGHT/ENHANCED: Headman and Wide-wing Passing

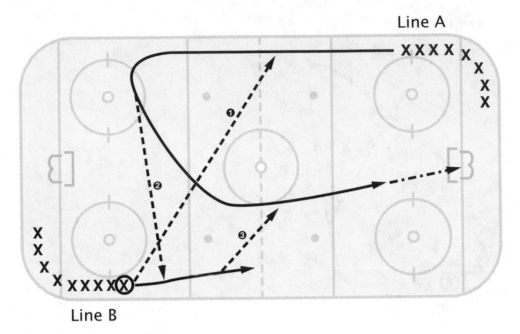

DESCRIPTION OF DRILL:
- The drill illustrated above involves three passes, two of which are positionally oriented. We are trying to teach the notion of spotting and passing to the wide wing in the neutral zone as well as the importance of headmanning the puck to teammates ahead of the puck carrier on the attack.
- Align the players in the corners as shown and on the whistle, one lead player will break into the neutral zone to receive the first of three passes to be made. This is the "wide-wing" pass, so the receiver should hug the boards and remain in the proper lane for a wing.
- They will then curl around the faceoff circle's edge as shown, passing across to the other line. After the pass, they are to break into the neutral zone, returning to the zone they originated from and they will receive a headman pass. Take it in and shoot.

COACHING POINTS
Note that pass #2 is a tactical pass, too, in that the player from Line A must hit the man breaking out of the zone in order to receive the return headman pass. The player in Line B then initiates the mirror of the drill going the other way.

NAME OF DRILL: 4-on-0 to 2-on-2 Transition
SKILL TO BE TAUGHT/ENHANCED: Transition: 2-on-2 Offense/Defense

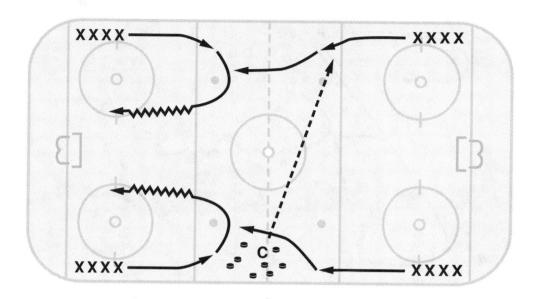

DESCRIPTION OF DRILL:
- Align players in all four corners as shown.
- On whistle, all four lines will send out their first player and coach will pass puck to whomever he feels deserves it.
- On receipt of pass, the receiving player and his partner will attack the other two players who have reverted to backskating and a defensive mode.

NAME OF DRILL: 3-on-1 Breakout Rush
SKILL TO BE TAUGHT/ENHANCED: Breakouts, Transition, Timing and Support

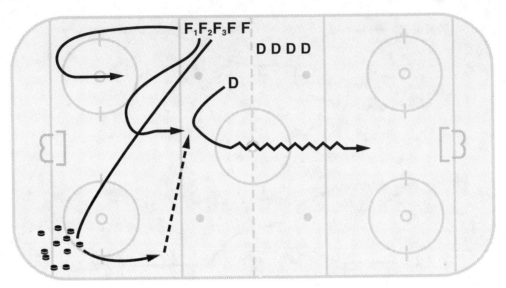

DESCRIPTION OF DRILL:
- Place the pucks in a corner opposite your line of forwards who are set at the far blue line alongside a line of defensemen, as shown.
- Forward #1 will curl to the base of the near circle, gaining his lane while forward #2 curls into the slot and forward #3 breaks into the corner to pick up the puck.
- Forward #3 outlet passes to #2 and then all three forwards break up ice against the lone defenseman who has begun his backchecking when forward #3 first touched the puck.

NAME OF DRILL: 3-on-2 Breakout Rush
SKILL TO BE TAUGHT/ENHANCED: Breakouts, Transition, Timing, and Support

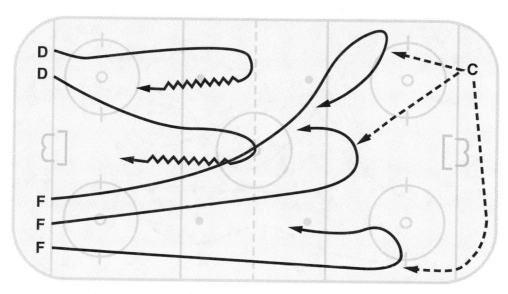

DESCRIPTION OF DRILL:
- Align a pair of defensemen in one corner and a set of three forwards in the other. Place a coach or designated passer in the corner opposite the defensemen, as shown.
- On the whistle, the three forwards break up ice to the far defensive zone where there they will curl, receive an outlet pass and return up ice to the attacking zone. Full speed must be emphasized.
- The two defensemen will begin their pattern when the forwards reach the far blue line.

COACHING POINTS:
- This drill can be mirrored with two defensemen and three attackers in the opposite corners. It is a high-speed, high-tempo drill.
- The coach initiating the breakout has the option of passing to any of the three forwards.

NAME OF DRILL: Manzione Transition Drill
SKILL TO BE TAUGHT/ENHANCED: Skating, Passing and Shooting;
Transition

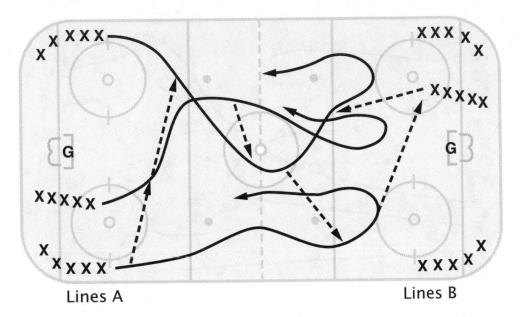

Lines A   Lines B

DESCRIPTION OF DRILL:
- Align players in three lines at each end of the ice.
- Three players will break out from one end, designated here as Lines A.
  They will skate through the neutral zone at high speed and, as coach
  Lou Manzione so often says, "being creative." Upon reaching one end of
  the ice, the player who last has the puck will dump off to any player in
  Line B.
- Line B will immediately outlet to any player in Lines A and then break
  up ice on their own 3-on-0 to mirror the drill.
- Lines A will complete their "shift" with a shot on goal.

COACHING POINTS:
Lou Manzione is a coach and administrator from the Brick Hockey Club
in central New Jersey.

NAME OF DRILL: 4-Pass Transition Drill
SKILL TO BE TAUGHT/ENHANCED: Passing

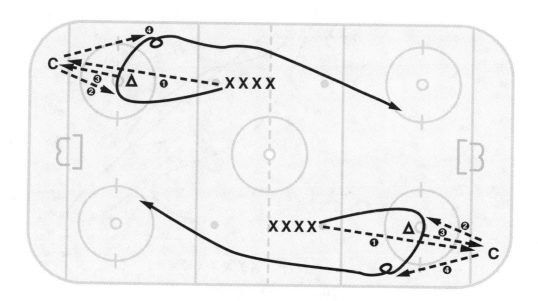

DESCRIPTION OF DRILL:
- Place a coach in each of two adjacent corners and line the players in the neutral zone as shown.
- The lead player in each line, on the whistle, will send a long dump-in pass to the coach and then he/she will break for the cone.
- Rounding the cone, the player and the coach will execute two one-timed tap passes (#2, #3).
- The coach, now with a puck after the third pass, will outlet up the boards to the skater breaking out. Note that the skater must pivot to face the coach for the pass. He/she will then spin out of the pivot and break up ice for a shot on goal.
- Use both ends of the ice simultaneously.

NAME OF DRILL: 3-0/3-1 Transition Drill
SKILL TO BE TAUGHT/ENHANCED: Skating, Passing, Playing the 3-1

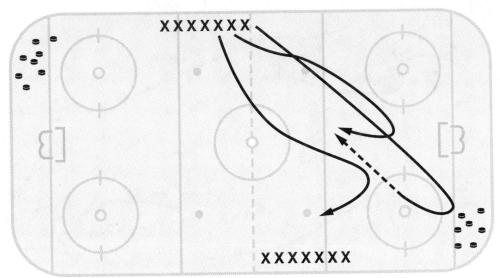

Phase I: Outletting

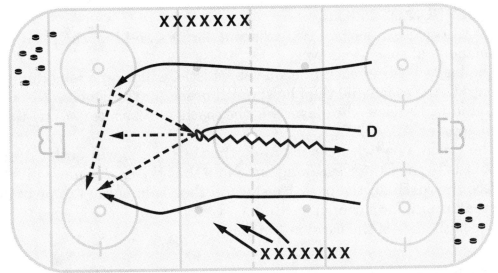

Phase II: 3-0 Rush; Defense Prepares to Face a 3-1

DESCRIPTION OF DRILL:
- Players are lined up in the neutral zone and pucks are lying in the corner, as shown.
- On the whistle, the first three players will break into the defensive

zone with a defenseman in the lead. The defenseman picks up a loose puck, outlets to a forward of his/her choice and joins a 3-on-3 rush. However, the defenseman will only rush to his/her point position.

- Once a shot is taken, the leading three players on the opposite line will replicate the drill coming back as a 3-on-0 against the defenseman who rushed to his/her point position.

NAME OF DRILL: Doyle's Breakout Drill
SKILL TO BE TAUGHT/ENHANCED: Breakout Passing

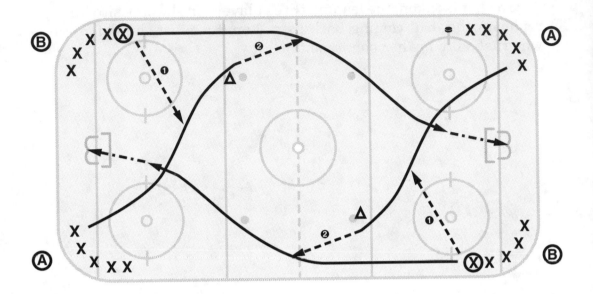

DESCRIPTION OF DRILL:
• Align the players in four corners, each with pucks.
• Players from Line A will break across the defensive zone and receive a breakout pass from the lead players in Line B.
• Line A players will then slide a quick diagonal pass once they reach the cone to the passer from Line B who broke up the boards after having outletted the pass. Line B players can then skate in for a shot on goal.
• Switch sides after a few minutes.
• Line A players, after passing, will join their opposite line A.
• Note how Lines A and B configure with Line A players facing the endboards.

COACHING POINTS:
This drill is named after coaching colleague Pat Doyle of the Brick Hockey Club in central New Jersey. He credits former Lake Superior State coach Frank Anzallone with the drill.

NAME OF DRILL: 5-0 to 3-2 Transition
SKILL TO BE TAUGHT/ENHANCED: Breakouts and Offensive Patterns

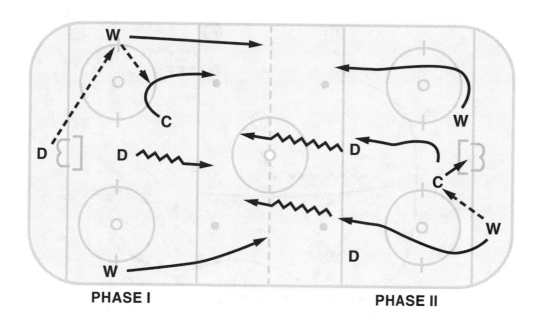

PHASE I   **PHASE II**

DESCRIPTION OF DRILL:
Diagrammed in two phases:
1. Team breaks out of defensive zone 5-0 (can use any variety of called breakout plays).
2. Once shot on goal is taken, forwards return back up ice 3-2 as defensemen begin backskating from their points.
• A variation on this drill is to have the initial breakout with five players attack two defensemen on a 5-2. The two defenders will, after the shot is taken, join the forwards on a rush/breakout back up the ice attacking 5-2 vs. the other defensemen.

COACHING POINTS:
• This drill can be used effectively in only 1/3 of the ice. Once the forwards clear the blue line, have them return back into a 3-2 vs. their defensemen.
• Coaches can incorporate all of the breakout schemata they employ by calling for each play prior to dumping the puck into the zone.
• The 1/3-ice version of this drill is used by Princeton University as part of their warm-up/pregame series.

NAME OF DRILL: Defense/Offense Transition
SKILL TO BE TAUGHT/ENHANCED: Coordinating Wing and
Defenseman

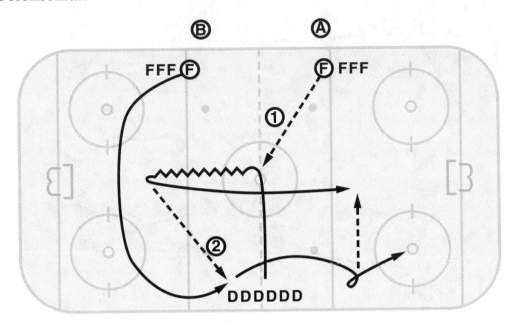

DESCRIPTION OF DRILL:

- Align defensemen in the neutral zone and forwards along the far boards as shown. The forwards have the pucks.
- The defenseman initiates the drill by breaking along the red line and receiving a pass from the forwards in Line A. He/she will then pivot into a backskate mode.
- In the meantime, the forward in Line B has looped back into the defensive zone and then up the boards for an outlet pass.
- Both will attack 2-0.
- Mirror the play going back the other way.

COACHING POINTS:

- In the attack sequence, have the forward execute a "turn-up" once he/she crosses the blue line and allow the defenseman trailing to get into the rush. You may also prefer to have the forward continue the rush into the corner and utilize the defenseman in a true trailer play.
- The diagram shows the turn-up.

NAME OF DRILL: Four-Corner Overspeed
SKILL TO BE TAUGHT/ENHANCED: Hi-Tempo Acceleration, Passing,
Shooting

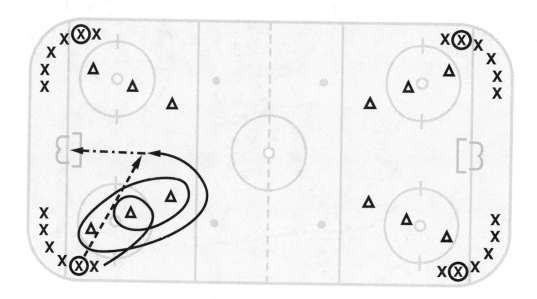

DESCRIPTION OF DRILL:
- Use all four corners at once, but alternate sides in each end.
- The lead player in each line will loop the second cone, far cone and near
  cone in quick succession en route to the goal. Coming out of the third
  turn they will receive a pass from the second player in line who then
  breaks after releasing the pass.
- Finish with a shot on goal.
- Note the angular positioning of the three cones.

COACHING POINTS
"Overspeed" is a European skating concept that calls for quick feet, high-
tempo acceleration and so forth. In short, it means that each player must
challenge him or herself to skate faster than they think they can. Allow
for no gliding patterns or gentle, loping turns.

NAME OF DRILL: Hi-Tempo 3-on-3
SKILL TO BE TAUGHT/ENHANCED: Passing, Skating

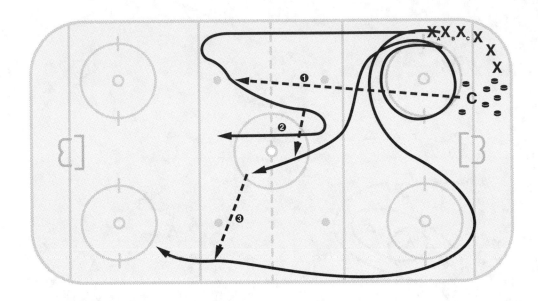

DESCRIPTION OF DRILL:
- Taken from Dartmouth assistant coach Rob Abel's drillbook, he calls this the Blatherwick 3-0 named after the former US Olympic coach. It is an excellent high-speed drill for advanced players.
- Place a coach with pucks on the goalline as shown. On the whistle, three players will break out.
- Player A breaks hard along the boards to the far blue line where he/she curls back for a pass from the coach (#1). Player B skates one lap around the near faceoff circle and then heads up ice, while player C skates an "S" around both circles and similarly breaks up ice. A 3-on-0 ensues.

NAME OF DRILL: Two-Man Transition
SKILL TO BE TAUGHT/ENHANCED: Passing, Support, 1-1 Play

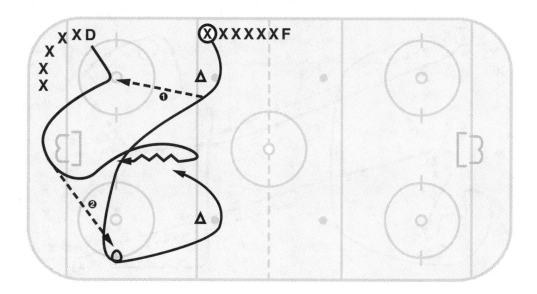

DESCRIPTION OF DRILL:
- Align forwards in the neutral zone, with pucks, and defensemen in the corners as shown. Both ends of the ice can be used simultaneously.
- On command, the first forward rounds the near cone and breaks into the offensive zone. He/she will not shoot, however. They will pass off to a defenseman who has broken to the dot.
- The defenseman will carry around the net and pass off to the forward who has crossed the ice to his breakout position, seeing this same zone as a defensive zone now. The wing will receive the outlet pass, skate around the cone and return into the zone facing a 1-on-1 with the defenseman who had rushed to the blue line, pivoted into a backskate mode, and is now an opponent.

NAME OF DRILL: 2-0 ISO
SKILL TO BE TAUGHT/ENHANCED: Forcing Offensive Zone 2-0 in
Exploitative Situations, Long Passes

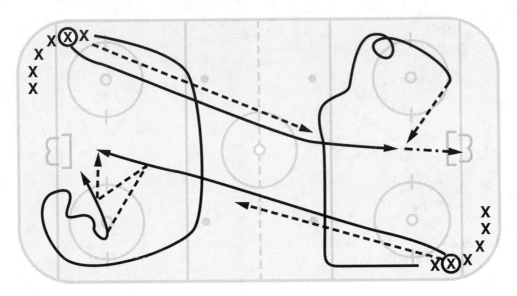

DESCRIPTION OF DRILL:
- This is an advanced drill that will: A) teach players to look for long
  breakout passes when opportunities arise, and B) teach players to overload a zone with 2-0 play (i.e., Wayne Gretzky said that offensive hockey
  is essentially the creation of 2-1's against individual players). This will
  be especially helpful to coaches who wish to exploit a weak defenseman
  in a game.
- Players set up in opposite corners.
- First player skates along his near blue and receives pass from 2nd
  player in opposite corner. The player who just passed breaks into offensive zone while pass recipient "rags" puck into corner, patiently
  waiting to set up 2-0.

COACHING POINTS:
You can make this interesting by adding the third player on line as a
defender, thus creating a 2-1.

NAME OF DRILL: Backskate Support Drill
SKILL TO BE TAUGHT/ENHANCED: Backskating, Passing, Support

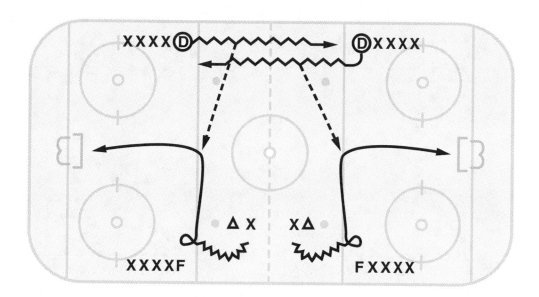

DESCRIPTION OF DRILL:
- Defensemen line up along the boards as shown, forwards align oppo-site them along the other boards. Both groups will employ the back-ward cross-under acceleration technique to begin skating.
- On the whistle, the defensemen begin to backskate with pucks and they will pass to the supporting forward once they are open along the blue line. Often, the defensemen will have to pass off their backhand and this is to be encouraged.
- On the same whistle, the forward will accelerate in their backskating around the cone, pivot to a foreskating mode, receive the pass and cut in for a shot on goal. Note that they have stepped up to align them-selves by the cone to begin the drill. This helps with the timing ele-ment.

COACHING POINTS:
- The forwards and defensemen should switch passing lines, as a group, at a given point during the drill since skills learned at either end will be helpful for each position.
- The coach should emphasize that this drill illustrated the need for "cutting to the pass."

NAME OF DRILL: Triangular Fire Drill
SKILL TO BE TAUGHT/ENHANCED: One-Timed Passing and Shooting

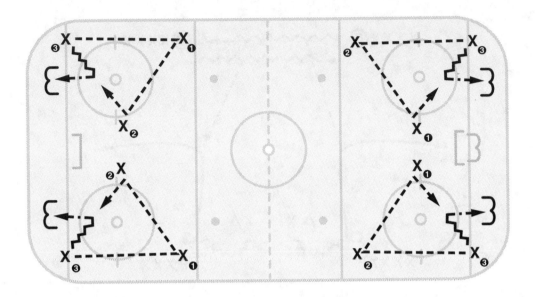

DESCRIPTION OF DRILL:
• If possible, use four nets and four groups of players.
• The corner man, player 3, passes to the point who then sharply passes to the man on the faceoff circle's edge, player 2.
• Player 2 one-times a pass to the initial passer from the corner who, after having passed to the pointman, has broken for the slot. He, in turn, one-times a shot on goal.
• Rotate the triangle in numbered sequence (1 goes to 2, 2 goes 3 and 3 goes to 1).

COACHING POINTS:
• This drill is an excellent reaction drill for the goalie, too.
• Coaches may wish to ask their pointmen to fake the shot and then pass off. This is a helpful skill that they must learn.

NAME OF DRILL: Hug The Line (and Stay Onside)
SKILL TO BE TAUGHT/ENHANCED: Offensive Skills

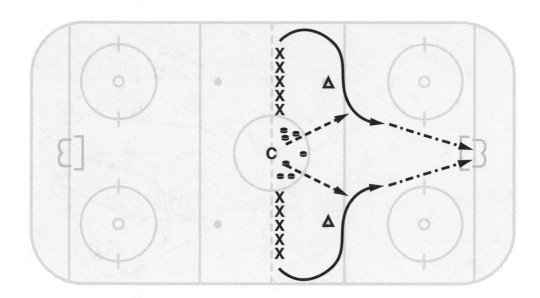

DESCRIPTION OF DRILL:
- Set a cone at each neutral zone faceoff dot and line your forwards along the red line. The coach is in the circle with pucks.
- One player goes at a time, but this drill should be replicated at both ends of the ice simultaneously.
- On the signal one player will dash around the cone and hug the blue line skating parallel or straddling the line until they receive the headman pass from the coach. At this point they will cut in for the shot on goal.

COACHING POINTS:
- A central point being taught in this drill is what to do when you are ahead of the play in the neutral zone — keep skating, stay onside and get open!
- Upon receiving the pass, have them execute a cross-over step to reaccelerate into the offensive zone.

NAME OF DRILL: Quick-Break Drill
SKILL TO BE TAUGHT/ENHANCED: Breakouts, Support

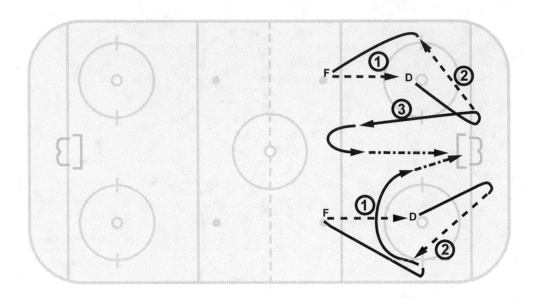

DESCRIPTION OF DRILL:
- Forwards, preferably wingers, line up at the blue line while defensemen begin the drill from the endzone dots.
- On the whistle, the wing passes to the defenseman and breaks for his/her breakout position along the boards. He/she should be facing the defenseman who has received the pass and has skated toward his net.
- The puck-carrying defenseman breaks toward the cage, spins or stops sharply and turns to pass the puck off to the winger.
- Drill A shown above is that described above; drill B adds a third pass — one that teaches/drills the give-n-go breakout with defensemen.

COACHING POINTS:
- Use all four quadrants of the rink for this drill to maximize ice-surface usage.
- To complete the drill have the final pass recipient spin back toward the goal for a shot.

NAME OF DRILL: 3-on-3 Short Game
SKILL TO BE TAUGHT/ENHANCED: Tap Passing, Anticipation, Reading

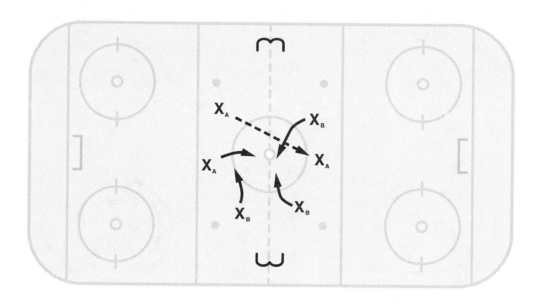

DESCRIPTION OF DRILL:
- Coach Red Gendron of the New Jersey Devils noted in a clinic that "little games" like the one described here are very beneficial because more things happen and they happen very quickly.
- Play 3-on-3 in the neutral zone with nets on the boards. Ask that all passes be one-timed tap passes. In this way, heads must be up, play must be anticipated and read and passes must be crisp.
- Perhaps add a dimension such as timing the number of passes or calling for three passes before a shot or timing the number of goals scored in one minute.
- Another key aspect of 3-on-3 "little games" is that of defense. Players must look to pickup "their man" or whomever is free and unchecked. This teaches good defense in a setting in which players are instructed to "pick up the loose change in front of the net."

NAME OF DRILL: Cycling Drill I
SKILL TO BE TAUGHT/ENHANCED: Cycling Concept, Passing

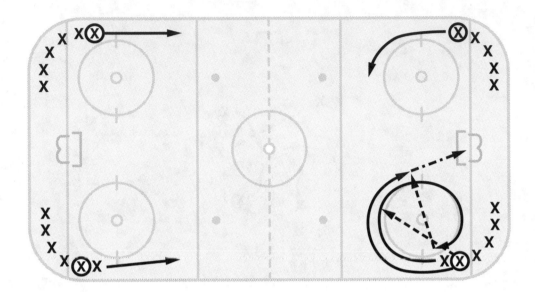

DESCRIPTION OF DRILL:
- Use all four corners at once for this drill, but alternate sides in each zone. The lead player in line breaks around the perimeter of the faceoff circle, receives a pass from the second player on line and then carries into the corner.
- The passer, after launching the pass, also breaks along the perimeter of the circle but he/she will receive a return pass from the corner. Take a shot on goal. Both players switch lines to the other corner.

NAME OF DRILL: Cycling Drills II
SKILL TO BE TAUGHT/ENHANCED: Offensive Zone Cycling

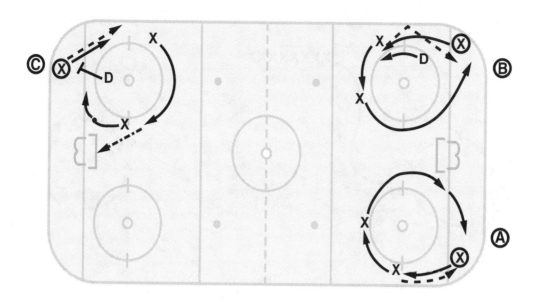

DESCRIPTION OF DRILL:

- Align sets of three players along the faceoff circles as shown. It is preferred that you use your regular lines for this drill as the players must learn the proper reads in order to properly cycle in the offensive zone.
- Basically, you will wheel around the perimeter of the circle in a cycling rotation. The objective is to draw the defenders out of position and create a good scoring opportunity. Begin the teaching progression by using drill (A). The puck begins in the corner and the carrier breaks up the boards only to dump it back off the boards to a trailer who has cycled into the corner.
- Now progress to cycle read (B). You will dump it back into the corner if the defender has skated up the boards with you. If the defender has remained in the corner by exerting pressure, pass the puck up the boards as shown in sequence (C).

COACHING POINTS:

When cycling up the boards and passing back into the corner, have the player spin/pivot and face the boards for a crisp, hard pass.

NAME OF DRILL: Cycling Drill III
SKILL TO BE TAUGHT/ENHANCED: Offensive Zone Cycling

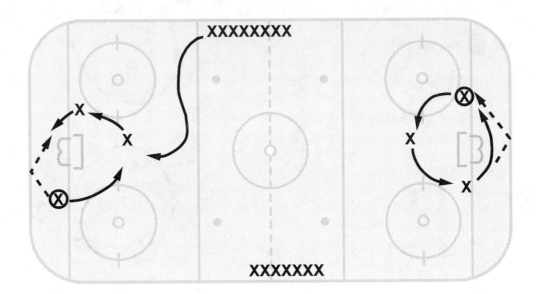

DESCRIPTION OF DRILL:
- Triangulate three players in front of the net as shown.
- On the whistle, they will cycle around the net, passing off the boards until a second whistle and then a shot on goal is allowed. You may wish to add a fourth attacker who jumps into the play as a pinching defenseman when the second whistle sounds. That player, trailing, will take the shot while the others position themselves for a rebound or screen/tip-in.
- Use both ends of the ice simultaneously.

NAME OF DRILL: Big Wheel Drill I
SKILL TO BE TAUGHT/ENHANCED: Passing; Support

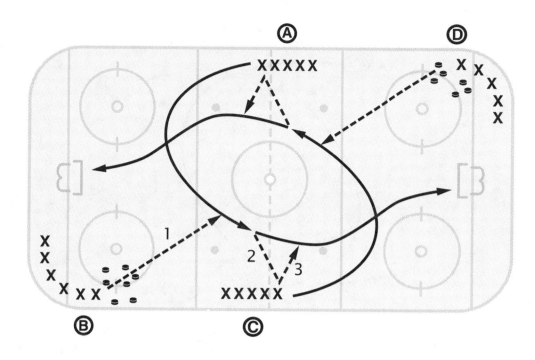

DESCRIPTION OF DRILL:
- It looks confusing, but it is a great skating and passing drill. Players also learn to come back into the defensive zone for support, too.
- Align the players in the corners and along the boards in the neutral zone, as shown.
- Begin the drill with the lead player in line A breaking into defensive zone, receiving pass from player in line B. Note that the lines in the corners have pucks; those in the neutral zone do not, initially anyway.
- The pass receiver from line A executes a give-n-go with the lead player in line C. Note that the return pass (shown here as pass #3) is a touch pass.
- After passing, the player in line C begins a mirrored route back into his defensive zone replicating the give-n-go just as the player in line A initially did. The player in line B who launched the breakout pass (shown as pass #1) merely steps up into line C after passing. After the shot, the players from lines C and A will merely join lines B and D in their respective corners.

NAME OF DRILL: Big Wheel Drill II
SKILL TO BE TAUGHT/ENHANCED: Support, Passing, Hi-Speed Dekes

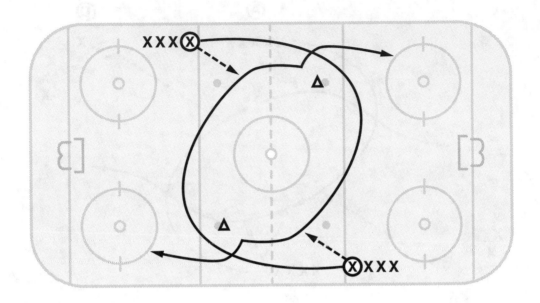

DESCRIPTION OF DRILL:
- Line up two rows of players at each blue line corner.
- Player skates out, around cone, receives pass from his opposite lined player.
- Repeat with other line.
- Can add shot on goal; can add cone deke.

COACHING POINTS:
Teaches player to break into openings and to buttonhook back into zones for support. Keep the passes to 15' or less.

NAME OF DRILL: Quick-Break Drill
SKILL TO BE TAUGHT/ENHANCED: Transition and Breakout Passes

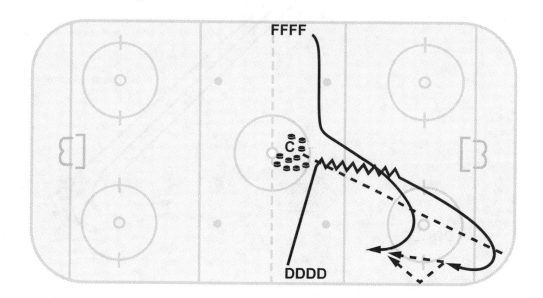

DESCRIPTION OF DRILL:
• Set forwards (F) on one side and defensemen (D) on the other as shown. Coach will set up in the circle with pucks. Begin the D line first.
• The coach will fire a puck into the corner nearest the D and both D and F will break as shown. D will reach the puck first because the puck was dumped in only when he/she had begun the backskating as shown. F comes back into the zone to support the D who then passes to F either directly or off the boards.

COACHING POINTS:
You can turn this into a 2-on-0 with the F dropping the puck back on a deep diagonal offensive zone tactical pass or you can make it a 1-on-1 with another D, on the line indicated, playing the attacker 1-on-1.

NAME OF DRILL: 3-on-0 to 3-on-0 Drill
SKILL TO BE TAUGHT/ENHANCED: Transitions, Passing, Breakouts

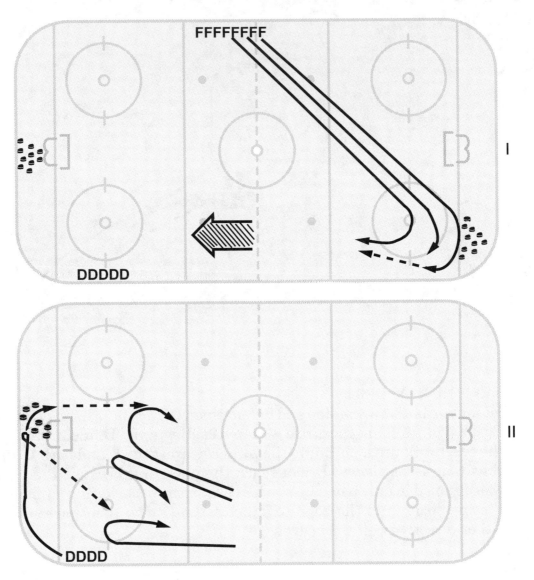

DESCRIPTION OF DRILL:
- Two phases to this drill are shown here.
- Phase I involves a simple 3-on-0 from the corner as shown.
- After taking a shot, Phase II kicks in with the defenseman breaking to pick up a puck behind the net and either spinning toward the boards to escape and pass out or carrying around the far side of the net to initiate another 3-on-0 with the same players going the opposite way.

COMBINATION SKILL DRILLS

"Intensity plus enthusiasm equals improvement, and improvement leads to success and confidence."

Coach Hubie Brown

NAME OF DRILL: Quick Feet/Quick Puck Drill
SKILL TO BE TAUGHT/ENHANCED: Skating Agility and One-Timed
Tap Passing
DURATION OF DRILL: 30 seconds

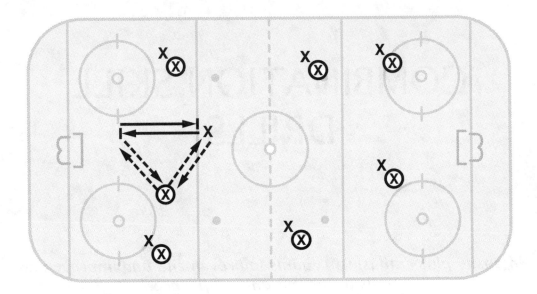

DESCRIPTION OF DRILL:
• Scatter players in pairs all over the ice. One player has the puck.
• On the whistle, the player with the puck is executing a series of side-to-side passes; he/she will remain stationary. The partner is doing the work by crossing over side-to-side quickly and tap-passing the return pass to the stationary player.

COACHING POINTS:
Quick feet!

NAME OF DRILL: Figure-8 Quick Passes
SKILL TO BE TAUGHT/ENHANCED: Skating Agility and One-Timed
Tap Passes

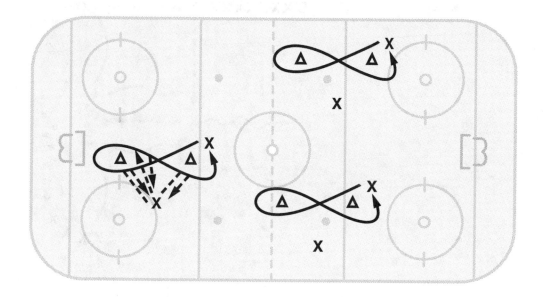

DESCRIPTION OF DRILL:
• Align pairs of players, with pucks near sets of cones as shown.
• On the whistle, one player, without a puck, will begin to weave a figure
  8-pattern in and about the cones, always facing the other player who is
  planted in front of him/her and with a puck.
• The stationary player is quickly passing the puck to the weaving player.
  Both are executing a series of one-timed tap passes.

COACHING POINTS:
Remind the weaving player to keep pivoting so that they face the passer
using backskate and foreskate modes.

NAME OF DRILL: Point Shot-Tip-In and 2-on-1
SKILL TO BE TAUGHT/ENHANCED: Passing, Shooting, Tip-Ins, Transition and Offense/Defense Skills

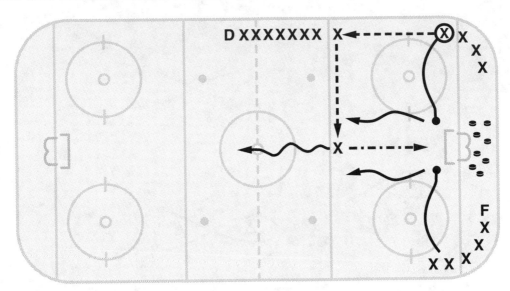

DESCRIPTION OF DRILL:
- This is a good combination drill which works a lot of facets of the game. Align forwards in the corners and defensemen in the neutral zone, setting two at the points.
- One forward will pass out to the point along the boards. Both corner forwards will then break for the cage (near the posts for a tip-in or rebound).
- The board pointman will pass over to the middle point who will take a low, hard shot on goal. He must create a tip-in opportunity or rebound.
- The forwards will tip the puck or shoot a rebound, but they only get one opportunity. They will then break out on a 2-on-1 against the shooting pointman, having picked up a loose puck near the net or the one they failed to put in.

NAME OF DRILL: Multi-Skill Attack Drill
SKILL TO BE TAUGHT/ENHANCED: Offensive Skills

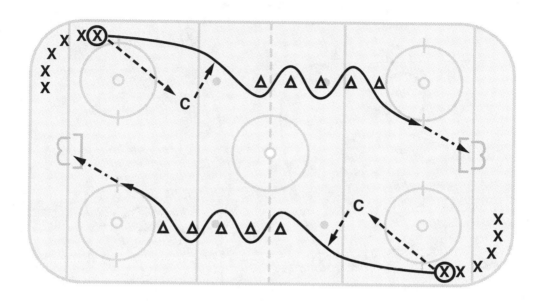

DESCRIPTION OF DRILL:
• Line the players in each corner and place a coach near each blue line.
• The drill begins with an outlet pass which turns into a give-n-go as the coach returns the pass. Do NOT let the player skate the puck out of the corner as they will want to do — this ruins the timing of the drill. Demand full speed on the break after the pass, too.
• The receiving player will carry the puck through the cones and finish with a shot on goal. Change lines when through.

COACHING POINTS:
If you have the puck carrier break to the outside of the first cone they attack, more dekes and a tighter turn at the final cone will be demanded.

NAME OF DRILL: "Drive To The Net" Multi-Drill
SKILL TO BE TAUGHT/ENHANCED: Board Passing, Shooting, Attacking The Net

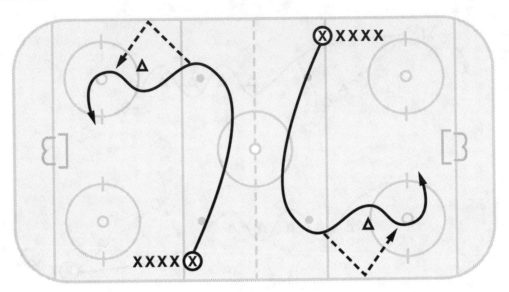

DESCRIPTION OF DRILL:
- Align players along the boards as shown.
- On the whistle, players break across the ice as indicated. They circle around the neutral zone faceoff dot and attack the cone with a board-pass to themselves.
- Once they pick up their own pass, they will find that the angle to the net is deep, so they must cut back into the slot at high speed and then get their shot off. Often times it will be a backhand shot, something that many players forget to use in low slot traffic.

NAME OF DRILL: 3-Skill Combo Drill
SKILL TO BE TAUGHT/ENHANCED: Passing, Stickhandling, Shooting

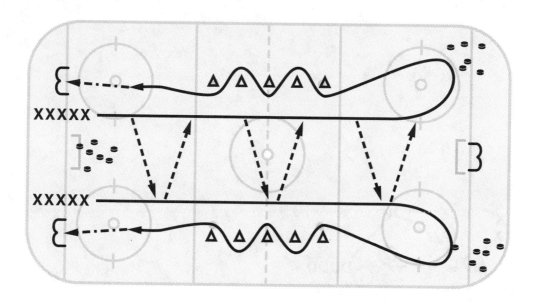

DESCRIPTION OF DRILL:

• Set pucks in two corners and one crease area. Align players in two lines adjacent to net with pucks in crease.
• Players begin rush down the ice with a 2-0, finishing with a shot on goal.
• Player on each side peels off to near corner, picks up loose puck and returns up ice through cones; finishes off with shot on goal.
• Note that three nets are needed; can work goalies in this drill.

NAME OF DRILL: Corner-Point Give-n-Go Drill
SKILL TO BE TAUGHT/ENHANCED: Coordinating Corner Wing and Pointman

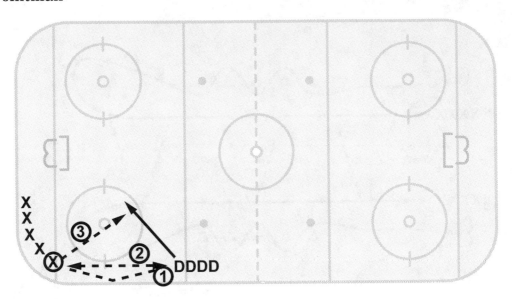

DESCRIPTION OF DRILL:
- Three passes will be employed in this drill.
- Begin with a winger in the corner with a puck. He/she will pass off the boards to the pointman who returns the pass back into the corner and then breaks for the net.
- A give-n-go is executed next (the third pass) as the defenseman pinches in as a trailer working his way in for the shot.
- Work all four corners, both ends and have the players switch lines to get the feel of either point. Alternate the shooting side, of course.

COACHING POINTS:
- This drill teaches not only board passing but also the concepts of give-n-go hockey and the use of the trailer man, in this case a defenseman who often can catch opponents by surprise with an offensive play like this.
- Cycling concepts can be reinforced in this drill, too, as you have the forward work his/her way to the point after the pointman walks in for the shot.

NAME OF DRILL: 2-0 / 2-1
SKILL TO BE TAUGHT/ENHANCED: Passing and 2-0 Combination Play

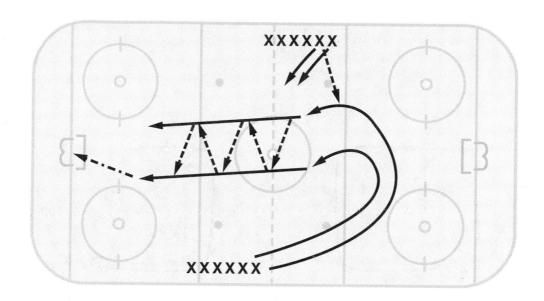

DESCRIPTION OF DRILL:
- Align players along boards in neutral zone.
- First two players break from the line and circle back into their defensive zone (one line at a time to begin the drill).
- The lead skater in the opposite line passes to one of the two skaters who is now coming out of the defensive zone. They receive the pass and head up ice 2-0.
- After passing, the passer and the next skater in line break into their defensive zone to replicate the drill going the opposite direction.

COACHING POINTS:
- This drill can easily be converted into a 2-1 sequence by having the passer drop into the neutral zone as a defender against the 2-0.
- FOR MORE ADVANCED PLAYERS: Add a timing element. For instance, whenever your line combinations are working 3-0, 2-0, 3-1, 3-2, 2-1 or 2-2, add in the equation that they must score within, say, 10 seconds. This adds tempo, competitiveness, crisp passing and quick-release shots.

NAME OF DRILL: Four-Pass Shooting Drill
SKILL TO BE TAUGHT/ENHANCED: Passing and Shooting

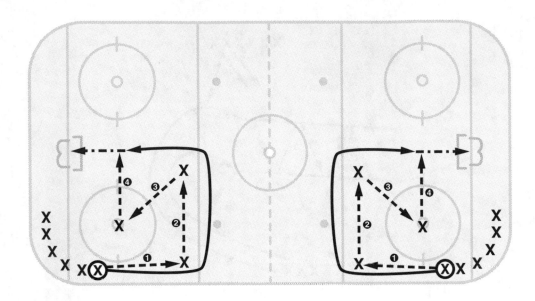

DESCRIPTION OF DRILL:
- Coaches can utilize all four corners if they choose for this drill.
- Line players in the corners with pucks. Also place a player at each point and one on the dot, as shown.
- The player in the corner will pass to the nearside pointman and loop in as indicated. Have them hug the blue line for about 15' before breaking in the for pass.
- The strongside pointman, after receiving the initial pass will pass off to the other point who, in turn, will pass to the man on the faceoff dot. That player will execute a one-time pass to the initial passer who should be knifing in for a shot on goal.

COACHING POINTS:
- The emphasis in this drill is for crisp, hard passing.
- After the shot, rotate the players or keep certain players in certain positions such as only defensemen to play the points, or a player who needs work on short passing to work the dot.
- Have players work one side of the ice and then shift to the other to get work on both backhand and forehand sides.

NAME OF DRILL: Cone-Cuts and 2-0's Drill
SKILL TO BE TAUGHT/ENHANCED: Puckhandling and Passing

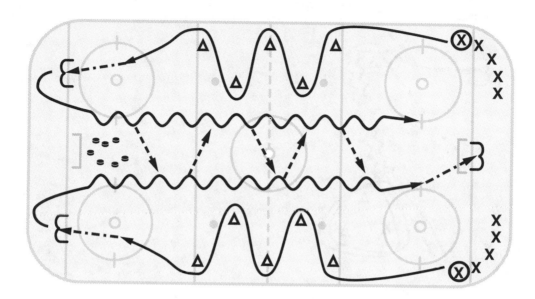

DESCRIPTION OF DRILL:

- Align players in corners as shown. The lead player in each line has a puck and upon the whistle will break into the cone-course weaving through it at high speed utilizing hard cuts and edge control as well as cupping the stick to control the puck in such hard cutting.
- Note how the cones are set at approximately 5-foot widths.
- End the first phase of this drill with a shot on goal after which the two players will return back up the ice working a 2-on-0 passing drill. This, too, ends in a shot on goal.
- Note placement of nets. You will need three. Also, place extra pucks in the "netless" crease so that players can pick one up to return up ice on the 2-0.
- Also note that this drill is similar to the one on page 45, but there is an important variation in the cone spacing. The angle of the cone alignments creates harder cuts, plus this drill finishes with a 2-on-0 rather than begins with one. You may even wish to incorporate a backskating 2-on-0, as is shown here.

NAME OF DRILL: Combo-Skill 2-On-0
SKILL TO BE TAUGHT/ENHANCED: Skating, Passing, Shooting

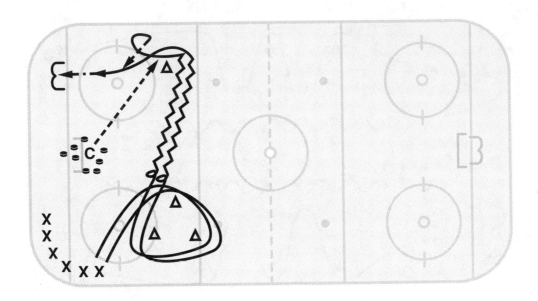

DESCRIPTION OF DRILL:

- Use both ends of the ice simultaneously for this multiple-skill drill. Align the players in the corner and place a coach, with pucks, in the crease. Off-set the net into the far corner.
- On the whistle, two players break at once, accelerate around the cone cluster, pivot into a backskate mode and backskate across the top of the slot to the far cone where they will pivot back into a foreskate mode.
- The first player to arrive at the far cone will take in a pass from the coach and then execute a Gretzky turn-up if time allows. They will eventually pass off to the other player streaking in toward the net.
- If both players arrive at the far cone together, the coach simply picks one player and a traditional 2-0 ensues.

CHECKING DRILLS

—Forechecking
—Body Checking
—Escaping the Puck
—Aggressiveness to the Puck

"Winning for the player or spectator is simply outscoring; for the winning team it is a way of talking about betterment, about making oneself, one's fellows, one's city, one's adherents, more noble because of a temporary engagement of a higher plane of human existence."

A. Bartlett Giamatti

NAME OF DRILL: Who's Gonna Score Drill I
SKILL TO BE TAUGHT/ENHANCED: Tenacity and Fighting Through the Checker

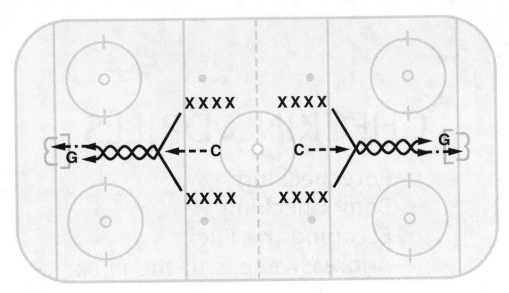

DESCRIPTION OF DRILL:
- Align the players on each side of the coach at the blue line.
- Coach will tap the puck forward and players, each of whom begins the drill on one knee, will race for the puck. Each tries to steal the puck and score in the same net.

NAME OF DRILL: Who's Gonna Score Drill II
SKILL TO BE TAUGHT/ENHANCED: Aggressiveness to the Puck

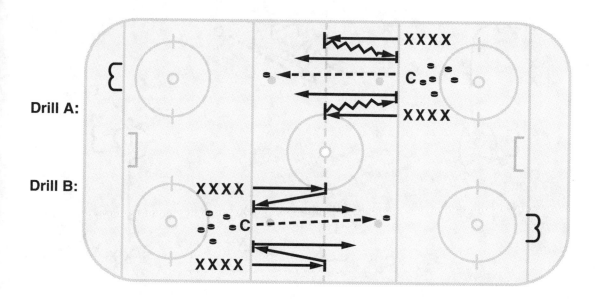

Drill A:

Drill B:

DESCRIPTION OF DRILL:
Essentially the same drill, here are two variations:
- In Drill A, two players in lines on either side of a coach with pucks will break for the red line, backskate to the near blue line, pivot and break up ice, racing for a puck that the coach has sent forward. One guy will win the puck while the other attempts to check him/her off it.
- Note that the nets are offset. Skaters should carry in for a shot on goal and then go to the other line for Drill B.
- In Drill B, the same skill is being imparted, but there is no backskate mode. Quickness, foreskate stops and aggressiveness are to be emphasized here. Have all stops face the same direction.

COACHING POINTS:
In Drill B emphasize the cross-over restart after the stop.

NAME OF DRILL: War In Front
SKILL TO BE TAUGHT/ENHANCED: Assertive Play in Front of the Net

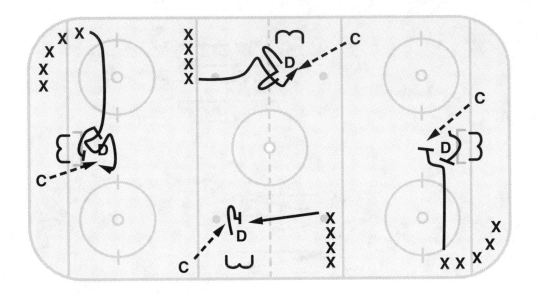

DESCRIPTION OF DRILL:

• Align players along sideboards, but keep one defenseman in front of the cage.

• On the whistle, the forward along the boards breaks to the front of the net where he will endeavor to "get open." Meanwhile, the defender is struggling to keep him covered and prevent a shot on goal.

• The coach has the pucks off to the side of the net and he or she will pass out only when the forward has gotten open by shaking off the checker.

COACHING POINTS:

• Set up nets in the neutral zone, too, and you can more effectively use the entire ice surface.

• Defensemen need to learn to play the body, so they should either be without sticks or holding them with the blade in their hand, upside down.

• Forwards need to learn to escape a checker in front of the net, so teach them to spin off the defender or sharply cross-check them away (avoid the penalty, of course, but in the technique taught here, the cross-check is designed to push the attacker away from the defender rather than knock the defender down which, of course, would draw the cross-check penalty).

NAME OF DRILL: Half-Ice One-On-One
SKILL TO BE TAUGHT/ENHANCED: Defensive Skills, Shaking Off
a Checker
DURATION OF DRILL: 20-30 seconds

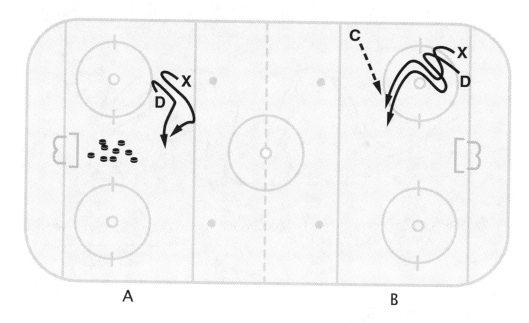

A   B

DESCRIPTION OF DRILL:
- Besides the more traditional linear 1-on-1 drill in which an attacker skates up ice and a defender retreats toward his net, here are two other "wrinkles" which can teach this fundamental skill.
A. Player D, without stick, keeps attacker away from pucks lying on ice behind him. Attacker's goal is, of course, to get to pucks and get as many shots on goal as possible in 20-30 seconds. Player D must play within rules!
B. Coach passes to attacker anywhere in zone, but should not do so until he has "shaken" free of checker. Defender is allowed use of stick in this variation.

COACHING POINTS:
Want to make them work? Try drill variation A with two stick-less defenders and one shooter!

NAME OF DRILL: Shadow Drill
SKILL TO BE TAUGHT/ENHANCED: Defensive Man-on-Man Coverage, Gap Control

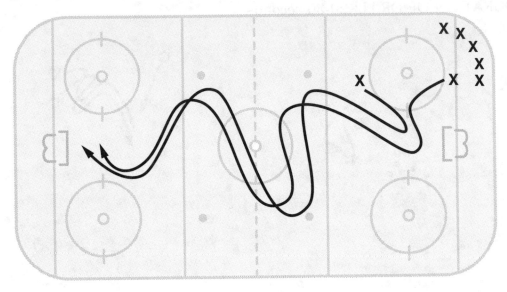

DESCRIPTION OF DRILL:
- Set players in lines in corners.
- First player sets atop circle, other player at base of circle. Player at top of circle begins to work his way, at will and in no set pattern, down the ice. Second player tries to maintain 5-10' inside-out leverage much like a defensive back in football covering a receiver.
- This drill can be worked with another set of players in other corner simultaneously.

COACHING POINTS:
- Have initiating player (at top of circle) buttonhook back into hashmarks to begin the drill; this allows shadowing player to pick him up.
- No pucks are necessary, but stick-to-stick poke-checking is encouraged.

NAME OF DRILL: Bust-a-Gut Backcheck Drill
SKILL TO BE TAUGHT/ENHANCED: Shooting and Then Backchecking

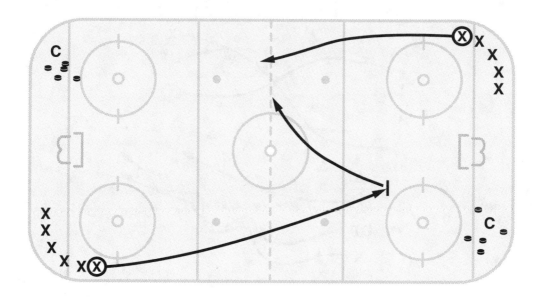

DESCRIPTION OF DRILL:
• Players align in corners as shown, each lead player with a puck.
• On the whistle, the first player will break down the ice for a shot on goal. As soon as the shot is released, the opposite player replicates the break up ice in the opposite direction. The player who first shot must jam on the brakes and work hard to get back to pick up the other player breaking up ice for his own shot on goal. Repeat.
• Work the hook and poke checks; dive if you must.
• Coaches are set near the nets with spare pucks to keep the drill flowing if the check is successful.

COACHING POINTS:
Teach the checkers to learn a proper cutoff angle.

NAME OF DRILL: 2-on-1 Backchecking
SKILL TO BE TAUGHT/ENHANCED: Forwards' Backchecking Skills

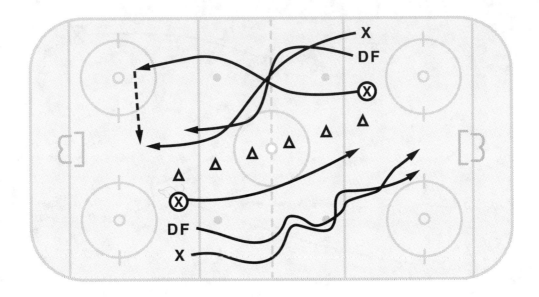

DESCRIPTION OF DRILL:
- Use cones to divide ice surface diagonally.
- Players break down ice in linear formation of three across; the defending forward is in the middle and he is to cover the non-puck carrying forward. They must stay onside and play within bounds of playing rules (i.e., no hooking, holding). The puck carrier will pass to his fellow attacker only if the latter breaks free of his coverage. The defender is trying to prevent this. Once in deep, the carrier may shoot while the other attacker goes for the rebound....unless the defender prevents this.

COACHING POINTS:
This drill literally shows the player what it means to "stay with his check," "shut down the passing lanes," or "pick up your man."

NAME OF DRILL: 3-on-3 Backchecking Drill
SKILL TO BE TAUGHT/ENHANCED: Defensive Skills for Forwards

Attackers

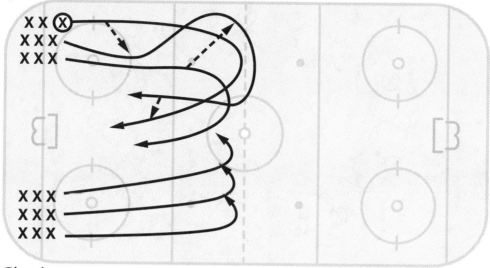

Checkers

DESCRIPTION OF DRILL:

- This is a simple yet highly important drill.
- Align sets of three skaters in lines in each corner. Both ends of the ice could be used simultaneously here.
- A 3-on-0 ensues from one corner while the other three forwards are assigned to cover "their man." Attackers must go to the red line; once they reach the line, the defenders break for the blue line and pick up their check.
- If one of the three attackers scores, ask whose fault it is.
- Switch lines after the drill is completed.

NAME OF DRILL: Poke-Check Drill (Forwards/Defense)
SKILL TO BE TAUGHT/ENHANCED: Poke-Checking Techniques

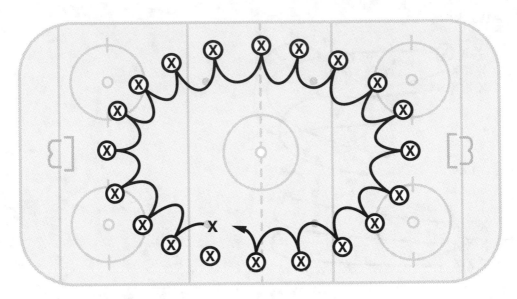

DESCRIPTION OF DRILL:

- Circle the players up in a huge, full-ice perimeter. Each stationary player has a puck and may not skate out of the check; they can only deke.
- Have one skater begin to circle the inside perimeter and attempt to poke the puck away with a one-handed poke-check. Emphasize the idea they he/she is to keep skating! (This gives the player the sense that they must attack the puck carrier from the side and regain position, all without stopping).
- Halfway around, begin another player around the perimeter so that time is efficiently utilized. (You may wish to have a player skate the perimeter as soon as his/her puck is poked away). When the first skater reaches the given starting point, the next player breaks out along the perimeter, poking and checking.

NAME OF DRILL: Pitbull Forechecking Drills
SKILL TO BE TAUGHT/ENHANCED: Forechecking Skills

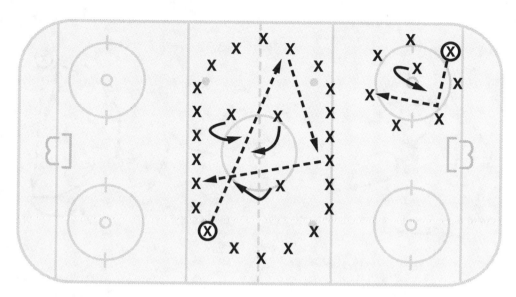

DESCRIPTION OF DRILL:
- Two variations on the same drill are shown here. One involves a full one-third of the ice; the other works in the confines of a single faceoff circle.
- In the circle drill use only one checker and have the players along the perimeter attempt to pass the puck across and around the circle. Depending upon the skill of the passers and the checker, the coach may wish to ask the check to use an inverted stick (i.e., the stickblade in the checker's hand).
- In the zone drill, set two or three checkers in the middle. You can add to the checkers by having anyone who has a pass intercepted join the checkers. You may wish to use two or even three pucks.
- Keep these drills lively and competitive.

COACHING POINTS:
Have the forecheckers read the EYES of the passers. Have them wave their sticks on the ice, too, to upset the timing and accuracy of the passers. Another good forechecking technique is to have the checker approach the puck carrier with his stick on the ice "showing one side" and then quickly whip it across to the other side on the first movement of the puck carrier's stick. It is critical that the checker have two hands on the stick in this maneuver.

NAME OF DRILL: 3-on-3 Forechecking Drill
SKILL TO BE TAUGHT/ENHANCED: Forechecking Systems Play

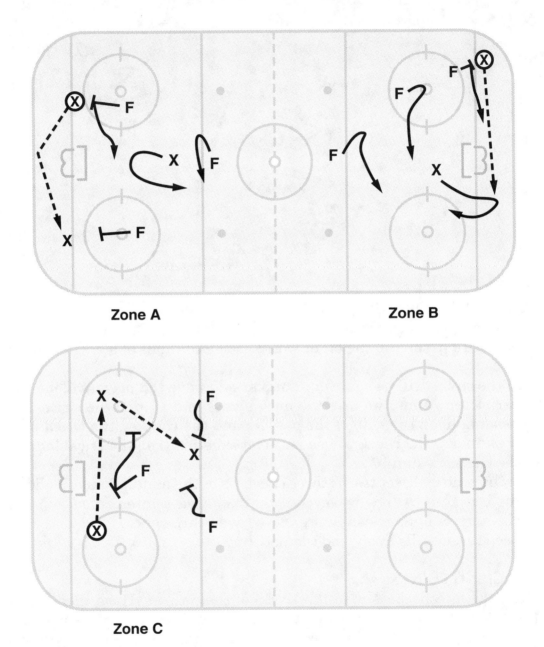

Zone A

Zone B

Zone C

DESCRIPTION OF DRILL:
- This drill will have to be modified to your system, but the general concepts of forechecking and reading the outlet passes are imparted here.

• If you send two men in, it is assumed that you keep one man high, or in the neighborhood of the blue line to pick off the outlet pass. Set defensive players in Zone A with a puck and have them work it between themselves or to the outlet man when he/she is freed up. Zone B shows an alternative system of two-men-in that is often used. Zone C, shown below, works off a one-man-in system..

• The system shown in Zone B calls for the nearest forechecker to attack the puck carrier while the backup man aligns himself on an imaginary line drawn from the puck to his own net. If the carrier escapes the leadman's check, the backup man attacks.

NAME OF DRILL: War In The Corners Drill
SKILL TO BE TAUGHT/ENHANCED: Corner Control, Mucking

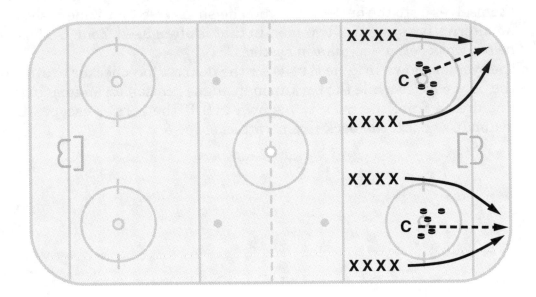

DESCRIPTION OF DRILL:
- Align players at the hashmarks in lines as shown. A coach is in the middle of two of the lines and he/she has pucks.
- The coach fires a puck into the corner and two players will chase it down. The winner emerges.
- Use both ends of the ice simultaneously.

NAME OF DRILL: Corner Drill
SKILL TO BE TAUGHT/ENHANCED: Checking and Escaping

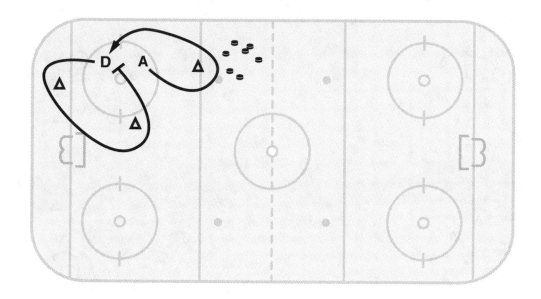

DESCRIPTION OF DRILL:
- Can use all four corners simultaneously.
- Offensive player and defensive player both begin inside a deep faceoff circle. At the whistle, they break around cones as shown. Attacker will pick up loose puck in neutral zone and break for the corner. He attempts to escape the check being offered by defender.

COACHING POINTS:
Teach defender to be patient and force attacker to outside. Play the body if age-group rules allow.

NAME OF DRILL: Corner Escapes
SKILL TO BE TAUGHT/ENHANCED: Puck Control, Defensive Pinning

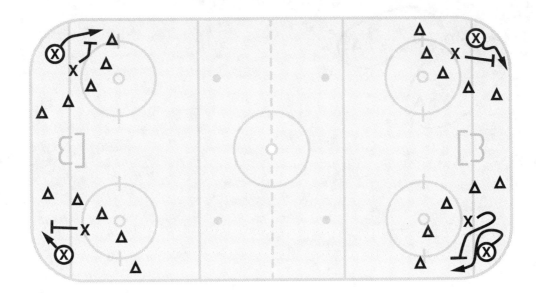

DESCRIPTION OF DRILL:
- Similar to the escape drill described elsewhere, this drill calls for the coach to set five cones in a semicircular fashion in each corner. Two players are then positioned inside the cones, one with the puck being nearest the corner boards. He tries to escape while the defender tries to check him against the boards.
- Have the defenders keep their sticks straight out in front of their bodies when making the initial attack. This takes away time and space more quickly.

COACHING POINTS:
- Young players will initially try to play the puck; they will soon learn to play the body.
- Control of the corners, especially the defensive corners to prevent the "walk-in" is critical to winning hockey.

NAME OF DRILL: 4-Circle Escape Drill
SKILL TO BE TAUGHT/ENHANCED: 1-1 Close-In Play Offensively and Defensively
DURATION OF DRILL: 10-15 seconds

DESCRIPTION OF DRILL:
• Defenders align on dot with blade of stick in hand (butt-end is on the ice).
• Puck carrier must escape from boards through circle.
• Body contact is allowed.
• Shot on goal can be allowed.

NAME OF DRILL: Checking I
SKILL TO BE TAUGHT/ENHANCED: Forechecking

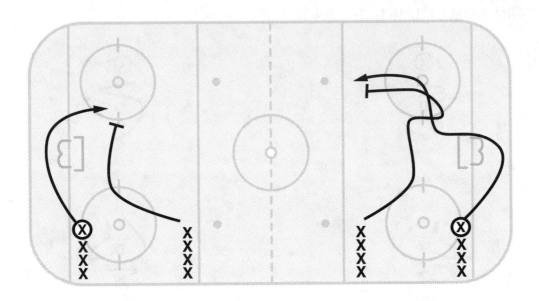

DESCRIPTION OF DRILL:
- Align players atop and below deep faceoff circles.
- Players on low end of circle have the puck and they are to break behind net and attempt to carry puck out of zone.
- Players atop circle are to break across face of net and "pinch them off" by forcing the puck carrier to the outside.

COACHING POINTS:
Be sure to work the players at both ends of the ice to ensure angle work from both sides.

NAME OF DRILL: Checking II
SKILL TO BE TAUGHT/ENHANCED: Forechecking

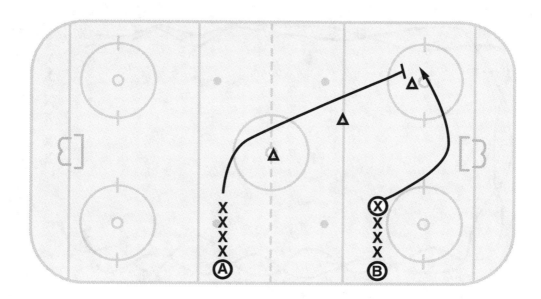

DESCRIPTION OF DRILL:
• Set up a diagonal of cones from the center-ice circle into the endzone
  dots. Players in line A will break down their lane and try to force the
  puck carriers from line B to the outside and/or steal the puck.
• Repeat on the other side.

NAME OF DRILL: Checking Drill III: Pinching
SKILL TO BE TAUGHT/ENHANCED: Elements of Checking

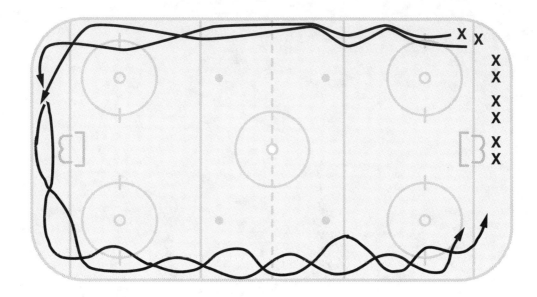

DESCRIPTION OF DRILL:
- Teach players how to receive the check first. In doing so, have them line up about 3-5' from the boards and skate into them. Teach them to "ride up" with the check, to brace themselves with an arm up (to protect the shoulders and offer a cushion to the impact) along the boards, and to absorb the hit by turning their hips and rolling with the impact.
- Having accomplished this, now teach the "pinch off" checking technique in which the checker angles the "checkee" off against the boards and pinches him or her off by driving the inside leg forward to cut them off. Employ a shoulder check, too.
- Drilling this requires teams of pairs or players circling the rink as shown. They are skating at half-speed and alternating in the role of "checker" and "checkee."

NAME OF DRILL: Checking Drill IV
SKILL TO BE TAUGHT/ENHANCED: Forechecking and Forcing the
Play

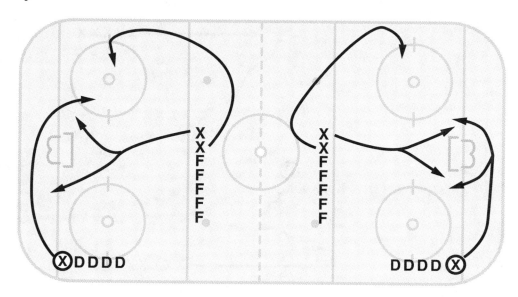

DESCRIPTION OF DRILL:
• Align forwards at the blue line and defensemen in the corners with the
  puck.
• Use both ends of the ice simultaneously.
• On the whistle, have the forward break into the offensive zone to pressure the defenseman with the puck. The latter has carried in behind
  his net and must escape to pass to the second forward who has curled
  to his breakout position along the boards.
• Teach the checking forward to read the defenseman's eyes and skating
  route. A timing element is involved here, too.
• If he is cut off in skating around his net, a good coaching point for the
  defenseman is to have him/her execute a tight hockey turn back toward the boards.

NAME OF DRILL: Defensive Angling Drills
SKILL TO BE TAUGHT/ENHANCED: Checking

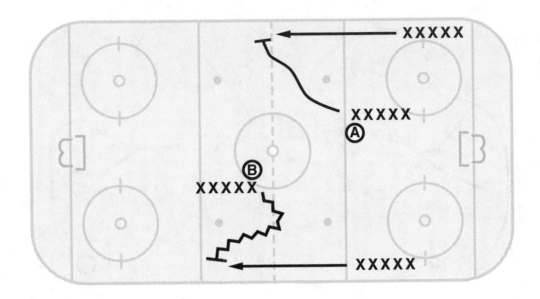

DESCRIPTION OF DRILL:
- Line up players as shown; forwards in Line A and defensemen in B.
- Teach defensive players to pinch attackers off at boards and force them to outside.
- Can add techniques such as "checking through the hands," hooking, stick-lift, hip-checks, etc.
- Teach your checkers that the aiming point for a puck carrier along the boards should be the carrier's hands.

COACHING POINTS:
- You may have to vary the placement of the lines based upon the skating abilities of your players. There is a timing element to this drill which will have to be fine-tuned by aligning the sets of players.
- "Checking through the hands" is a coaching point that calls for the checker, as he approaches a puck carrier along the boards, to aim his body/shoulder check at the hands of the carrier. In this way, the timing element will be more finely tuned and he will avoid being too far in front or behind the carrier.

NAME OF DRILL: Run The Gauntlet (III)
SKILL TO BE TAUGHT/ENHANCED: Balance, Taking the Check

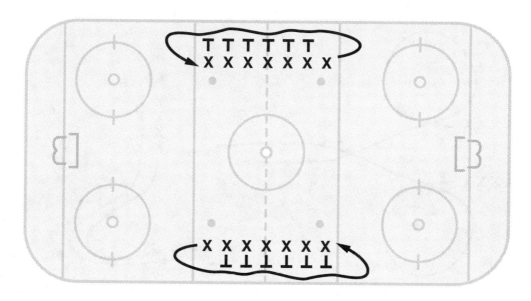

DESCRIPTION OF DRILL:
• Align two sets of players (more can be used, but the sets should consist of at least six players) along the boards.
• The player at one end of the line must, on the whistle, "bull" his/ her way through the others as they skate down the boards. The other players in line must provide at least moderate resistance.

NAME OF DRILL: Race For The Puck I and II
SKILL TO BE TAUGHT/ENHANCED: Recovery, Cross-Overs, Aggressiveness

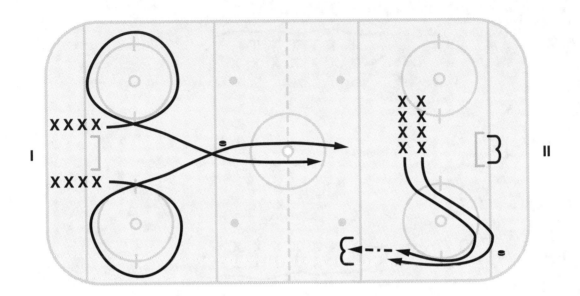

DESCRIPTION OF DRILL:

DRILL I: Players lie on stomachs alongside net. On the whistle, they spring to their feet, skate hard around the endzone faceoff circle to their respective side, accelerating as they go, and race to retrieve the single puck lying near the blue line as shown.

• The results include a breakaway, a fight for possession of the puck and/or backchecking skills.

DRILL II: Line players in front of the net, as shown, in two lines. On the whistle, they break for the corner to pick up and/or fight to obtain possession of the loose puck. The winner spins off and races for a breakaway with the other player hawking him or her all the way.

COACHING POINTS:

Emphasize aggressiveness to the puck and picking off the top hand on the puck carrier's stick when backchecking.

NAME OF DRILL: Race For The Puck III, IV, and V
SKILL TO BE TAUGHT/ENHANCED: Aggressiveness to Puck

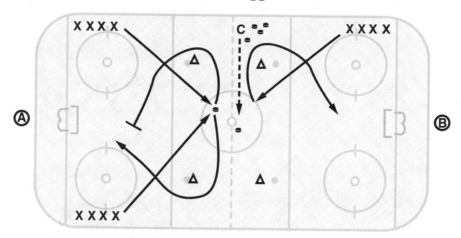

DESCRIPTION OF DRILL:
There are a variety of ways to execute this drill. Begin with a coach stationed along the boards to send pucks into the circle.

- In variant A, players dash from line, pick up puck and break in around cone for a shot on goal; other playeeer harries the carrier.
- In variant B, player dashes from line, picks up puck and loops back (either foreskating OR backskating) into zone around near cone.
- Variant C calls for the coach to drive one puck across the ice with two players chasing. Winner gains puck and attacks; loser hawks him/her in a backcheck mode. In this hi-speed drill, players begin from two lines in neutral zone along same boards they race along red line

In either case for variants A and B, single players are racing for the pucks at top speed. You may wish to ask the second player in line defend 1-on-1. (This is shown in variant A.)

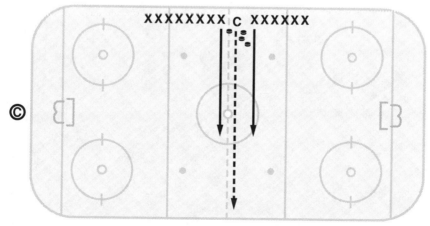

NAME OF DRILL: Race For The Puck VI
SKILL TO BE TAUGHT/ENHANCED: Aggressiveness and Skating

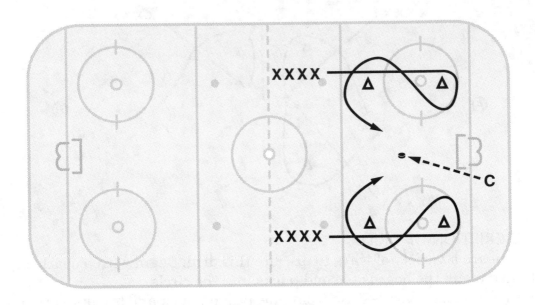

DESCRIPTION OF DRILL:
- This drill can be done at both ends of the ice simultaneously.
- On the whistle, the players break for a figure-8 course around the cones as shown. They will try to be the first to arrive in the slot.
- The coach will pass a puck out from the side of the net and into the slot where it will be picked up by the players racing for it.
- The "winning" player is expected to get a shot off while the "losing" player attempts to check him or her.
- Goalies should be used.

NAME OF DRILL: Race For The Puck VII
SKILL TO BE TAUGHT/ENHANCED: Speed Skating and Aggressiveness

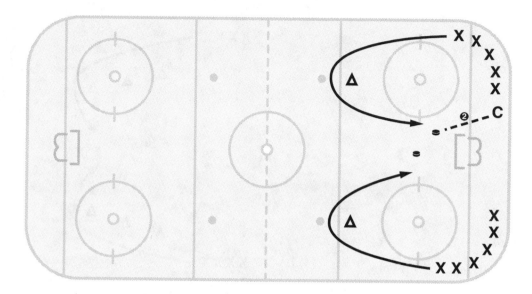

DESCRIPTION OF DRILL:
- Align players in corners as shown.
- On the whistle, a lead player from each line breaks for the cone near his/her blue line, circles it and skates hard for the loose puck. (A good variation of this drill is to have them skate backward to the cone as quickly as possible). The first person to the puck gets a shot, but the second person may receive a "rebound" (designated puck 2) passed out from behind the net by a waiting coach.

NAME OF DRILL: Race For The Puck VIII
SKILL TO BE TAUGHT/ENHANCED: Aggressiveness, Overspeed Training

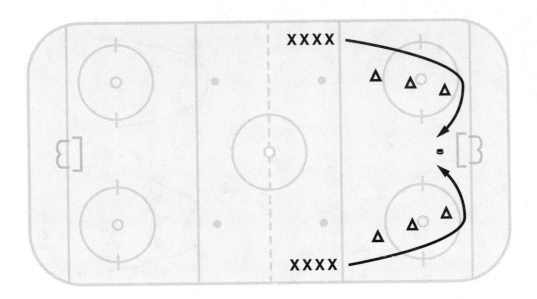

DESCRIPTION OF DRILL:
• Align players in two lines in the neutral zone as shown.
• Set cones up in one zone funneling the players toward the net.
• On the whistle, they will race for the puck and the first one arriving gets the privilege of a shot on goal.
• You can do two things with the player arriving late: A) tell them to go for the rebound; or B) tell them to act as a checker.
• Replicate the drill going the other way to utilize full ice or set up a 1-on-1 returning up ice.

NAME OF DRILL: Four-Check Drill
SKILL TO BE TAUGHT/ENHANCED: Defensive Zone Checking Skills for Forwards

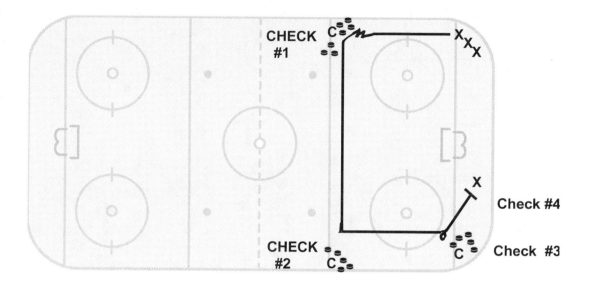

DESCRIPTION OF DRILL:

- Line players in one corner and have three coaches set at the points and in the opposite corner.
- On the whistle, the lead player breaks for the near point to execute a sliding block of a point shot. Note that the coach taking the shot may be using street hockey balls rather than pucks. This is Check #1.
- The player then scrambles to his feet to race across the ice to the other point where he will execute a poke check for Check #2.
- Check #3 calls for the player to drop to one knee and block a centering pass from the corner.
- Check #4 is a simple shoulder check against the last player in line, the player who just preceeded the checker.

COACHING POINTS:

- In executing the sliding shot-block, have the player slide just as he would in baseball but with both legs extended and stacked atop one another. He should aim the middle of his legpads in line with the puck. As for the centering pass-block, he should drop to one knee and have the stick extended in one hand out to one side in an attempt to maximize coverage.

ONE–ON–ONE DRILLS

"To get to the pinnacle, you have to keep working at it every single day and also have the passion for the business. You watch other coaches and pirate every bit of material you can, using it with a flavor of your own while being true to yourself and your ideals in terms of what makes you tick."

Coach Ted Sator

NAME OF DRILL: 1-on-1 Drill #1
SKILL TO BE TAUGHT/ENHANCED: 1-1 Isolation, Support and Breakout

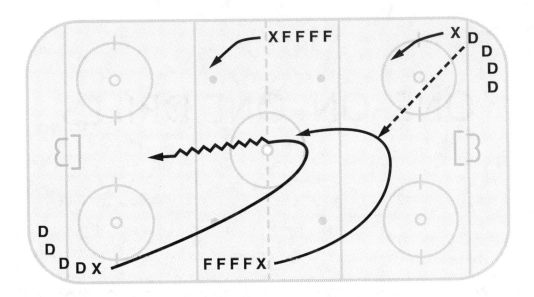

DESCRIPTION OF DRILL:

- There are many ways to initiate a 1-on-1 drill series, but this one is particularly effective because it makes skaters work at top speed. Moreover, it calls for backchecking support concepts, breakout passing and an emphasis on the defensemen picking the forward up at his defensive blue line.
- Align defensemen in the corners and forwards in neutral zone as shown.
- On the whistle, the forward breaks into the far defensive zone to receive the pass from the defenseman.
- Meanwhile, the rear defenseman also breaks on the whistle, but his objective is the far blue line. A 1-on-1 ensues.

COACHING POINTS:

Once this sequence is completed, blow the whistle again to signal a repeat of the drill from the other side.

NAME OF DRILL: 1-on-1 Drill #2
SKILL TO BE TAUGHT/ENHANCED: Attacking and Defending Skills 1-1

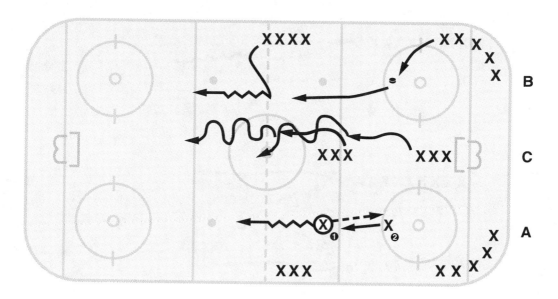

DESCRIPTION OF DRILL:
- This is a standard drill which can be initiated several ways, but here are three suggested methods:

A: Player 1 passes to player 2 to begin sequence with player 1 defending and 2 attacking.

B: Player 2 charges up ice and player 1 picks him at red line.

C: The player is performing the 1-1 drill without pucks and sticks to emphasize lateral movement and body control.

COACHING POINTS:
- Teach moves to attackers. Have them work specific moves on each attack — this should be directed by coach. Defenders must pick up the attackers by the defensive blue line to avoid "backing in."
- Coaches may wish to have defenders emphasize body contact by having them hold sticks with blade in hand (it is obviously more difficult to play the puck, hence less of an inclination to do so).

NAME OF DRILL: 1-on-1 Drill 3
SKILL TO BE TAUGHT/ENHANCED: Individual Skills Attacking and
Defending

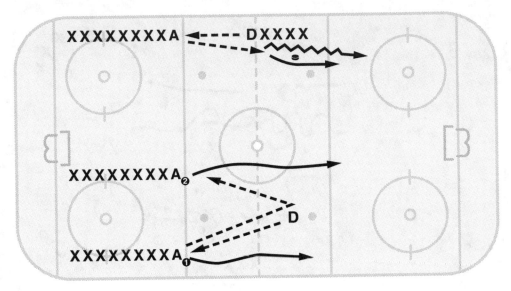

DESCRIPTION OF DRILL:
Here is another simple and innovative way to incorporate passing and
aggressiveness to the puck while setting up a 1-on-1:
- Defender (D) passes to attacker (A). He returns the pass to D who is
  backskating at that point.
- D simply leaves the puck where he receives it and allows A to break in,
  pick it up in full stride and attack 1-on-1.

COACHING POINTS:
A good variation off this drill is to create a 2-on-1 using tap passes as
shown in the variation (V) diagrammed above. D passes to Al who taps it
back to D who, in turn, taps it to A2. Both A-players will then break
toward D in a 2-on-1.

NAME OF DRILL: 1-on-1 Drill 4
SKILL TO BE TAUGHT/ENHANCED: Puck Control, 1-on-1 Attack/Defense

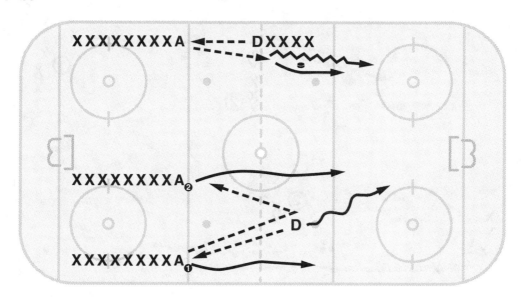

DESCRIPTION OF DRILL:

- Forwards line up along the boards and defensemen line up in center-ice faceoff circle as shown.
- On the whistle, the first forward will break through the neutral zone, across the blue line; he will receive a pass from the other line of forwards and then attack the defenseman 1-on-1.
- Once the pass recipient clear across the path of the other attacking line, the lead forward breaks and mirrors the drill pattern.

COACHING POINTS:

In any 1-on-1 situation, the defender must align on the attacker's inside shoulder to force him/her to the outside. Furthermore, they must focus their eyes on the attacker's navel rather than the puck to avoid biting on a deke.

NAME OF DRILL: 1-on-1 Drill #5
SKILL TO BE TAUGHT/ENHANCED: Hi-Speed Individual Skills

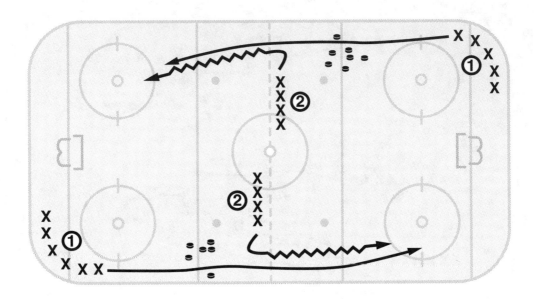

DESCRIPTION OF DRILL:
- In this variation two components are being emphasized — speed and coverage from the side of the attacker rather than facing him/her.
- Defensemen as well as forwards can play the defender's role here.
- Lines #1 will form in each corner while Lines #2 will set up at the red line.
- When the whistle blows, the lead skater in each Line #1 will break to pick up the loose puck on the blue line. As he/she touches the puck, the players in Line #2 will turn, backskate and defend. The speed of the players attacking should force the defender to fend the puck carrier off from the side, so the defender may have to pivot out of the backskating mode. This is not a problem. Emphasize the pinch to the outside and the one-handed poke.

NAME OF DRILL: 1-on-1 Drill #6
SKILL TO BE TAUGHT/ENHANCED: Individual Skills, Offense/Defense

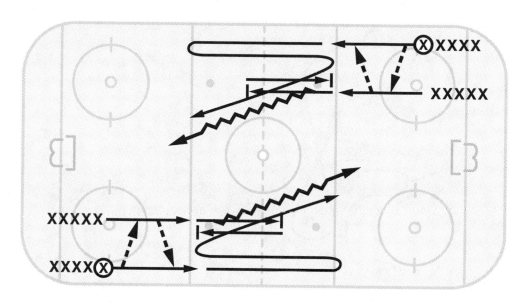

DESCRIPTION OF DRILL:

- Work both sides of the ice surface simultaneously. Align defenders on the inside lines and attackers on the outside lines. The players in the outside lines have the pucks.
- The outside lines initiate the drill by working 2-on-0 until they reach the neutral zone; by then the attacking player must have possession of the puck. He/she will break to the far blue line, pivot into a backskate mode and return to his/her near blue line, still with the puck.
- The defenders on the inside lines, after the 2-0 sequence will skate to the red line, jam on the brakes, crossover pivot and accelerate to the near blue line foreskating. They will then pivot into a backskate mode and pick up the attacker who should now be coming at him/her on a 1-1.

NAME OF DRILL: 1-on-1 Drill #7
SKILL TO BE TAUGHT/ENHANCED: Individual Skills, Offense/Defense

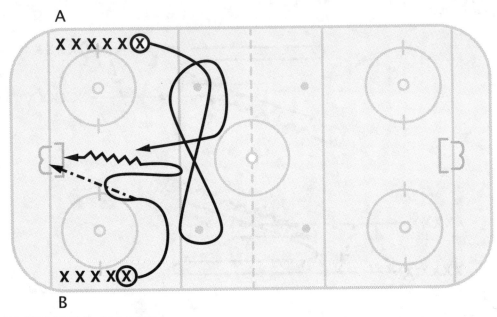

DESCRIPTION OF DRILL:
- This is a high-tempo drill in which the offensive players in Line A will execute a figure-8 puck-control set of turns in the neutral zone as shown. Meanwhile, the defensive players in Line B first attack the net for a shot on goal and then break to the blue line where they pick up the attacker to defend, 1-on-1.
- Since there is a timing element involved in this drill, it is recommended for more advanced players only.

NAME OF DRILL: 1-on-1 Drill #8
SKILL TO BE TAUGHT/ENHANCED: Individualized Attack/Defense
Drills

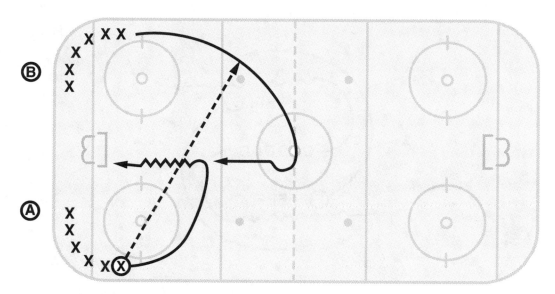

DESCRIPTION OF DRILL:
- Arguably, line A should be defensemen, but even forwards must need to work their 1-on-1 defending skills.
- Align players in the corners as shown. Line A will hit the lead skater in Line B with a cross-ice outlet pass and the Line B player, now with a puck will skate for the center-ice dot, turn and attack. The passer from Line A will have reached the blue line and must backskate to defend the 1-on-1.

NAME OF DRILL: 1-on-1 Drill #9
DURATION OF DRILL: Singular Offensive/Defensive Skills

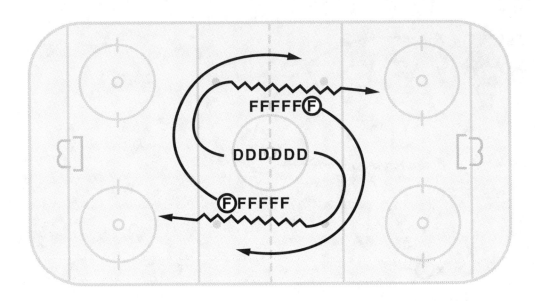

DESCRIPTION OF DRILL:
- Simple yet effective, this drill calls for the line of defensemen at center ice to break around the faceoff dot, pivot into a backskate mode and confront an attacker coming from the opposite lines as shown.
- Work both ends of the ice simultaneously and don't hesitate to work your forwards into the defensive mode of the 1-on-1 either, since you never know when an alert forward must backcheck and cover a defenseman who pinched in and was caught up ice!
- This drill puts considerable pressure on the defensemen to accelerate their backskating.

NAME OF DRILL: 1-on-1 Drill #10
SKILL TO BE TAUGHT/ENHANCED: Passing, Breakouts, and 1-On-1's

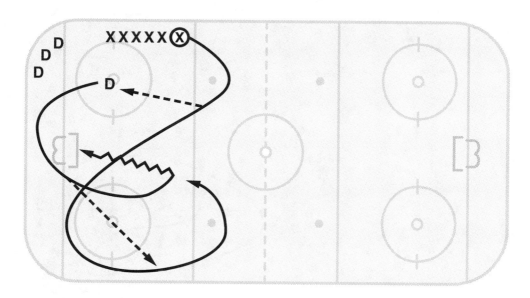

DESCRIPTION OF DRILL:
- Set defensemen in the corners and forwards near the blue line as shown. Use both ends of the ice simultaneously.
- The lead forward will, with a puck, break from his/her line to and around the near faceoff dot after which they will pass to a defenseman who has skated to the deep dot.
- The forward will continue around to the far boards and set up for a breakout pass which they will receive from the defenseman who carried behind his/her net for this purpose.
- The forward will then circle the other neutral zone faceoff dot and come back to attack the defenseman 1-on-1. Note that the defenseman, after the breakout pass, had skated to his/her near blue line and pivoted to a backskate mode to confront the attacker.

NAME OF DRILL: 2-0 to 1-1 Variation Drill
SKILL TO BE TAUGHT/ENHANCED: Close-Order Passing and 1-1 Defense/ Offense

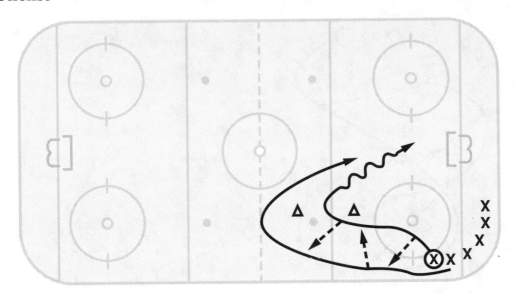

DESCRIPTION OF DRILL:
- Align players in all four corners (only one corner is shown above for the sake of clarity). Set two cones just inside and outside of the blue line, as shown.
- The player with the puck breaks up ice to the inside and executes a series of 2-on-0 passes with his/her partner. However, the outside player must have the puck by the time they reach the neutral zone.
- The puck carrier skates around the furthest cone and comes back to attack the inside player who has skated into a backskate mode after having pivoted around the lower cone. They work a 1-on-1.

NAME OF DRILL: Neutral Zone Support Drill
SKILL TO BE TAUGHT/ENHANCED: Support Concepts, Passing, 1-1

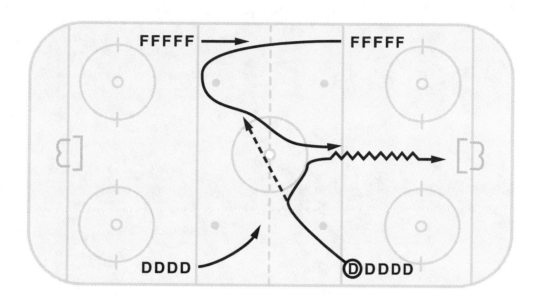

DESCRIPTION OF DRILL:
• Defensemen line up along one side while forwards align opposite them by the boards.
• The defenseman carries the puck to begin the drill; he/she skates toward the center-ice faceoff dot and passes to the forward who...
• Curls toward him after gaining the blue line, receives the pass and then attacks the defenseman one-on-one who...
• After having passed the puck off, backskates.
• Replicate the drill going the other way to utilize full ice.

POSITIONAL SKILL DRILLS
–Defensemen
–Forwards
— Skills Related to Specific Positions

"It would not be an exaggeration to say that how a team plays tells you something about the coach."

Coach Darryl Sutter

NAME OF DRILL: 3-Zone Specialty Drills
SKILL TO BE TAUGHT/ENHANCED: Skills Related to Specialized Positions

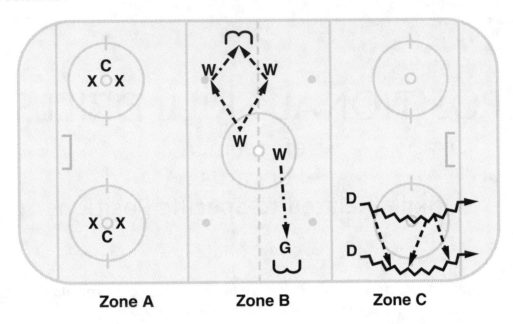

Zone A   **Zone B**   **Zone C**

DESCRIPTION OF DRILL:
There will come a time in your season when you must address skills relevant to special positions. Here's a way to approach this dilemma.
- In Zone A, centers are working faceoffs.
- In Zone B, wingers are working on their shots against target boards, live goalies, or even special shots against open nets (for example, have them work snap shooting or tip-ins).
- In Zone C, defensemen are working on backskating puck control and passing as well as point shots. They could also be working on the timing element regarding when to drop to the ice to block a pass or shot.

NAME OF DRILL: Point/Pivot Drill
SKILL TO BE TAUGHT/ENHANCED: Backskating with Puck, Pivot and Shoot

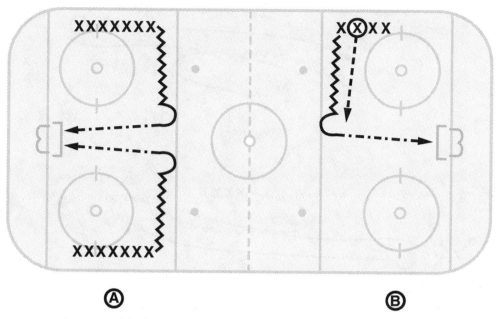

DESCRIPTION OF DRILL:
There are 2 good variations on this drill:
- Drill A: Players line up along blue line at "point" with pucks. They backskate with puck to middle-point position, pivot and shoot on net.
- Drill B: Players backskate without pucks and receive it from second player in line once they reach the middle-point position. They pivot and shoot.

COACHING POINTS:
- In teaching the drill, it will be easier to have left-handed shots on the left point and right-handed shots on the right point.
- Each side can be worked simultaneously as in Drill A.

NAME OF DRILL: Defenseman's Pressure Drill
SKILL TO BE TAUGHT/ENHANCED: Defending the 1-1, 2-1 Under
Pressure of Speed and Time

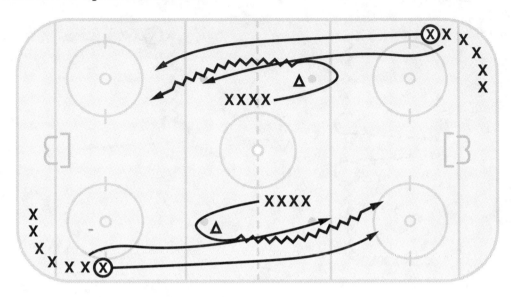

DESCRIPTION OF DRILL:
- Align forwards in the corner with pucks and the defensemen along the
  dots in the neutral zone as shown.
- The top half of the diagram illustrates a 1-1 in which the defenseman
  must break for the cone, pivot to the outside and into a backskate
  mode to face the attacking forward who also broke on the same whistle.
- The bottom half of the diagram shows a 2-1; simply have two forwards
  break.
- The timing of this drill is acute since the forwards will arrive in the
  face of the defender very quickly after the pivot. The defenseman had
  better "move his feet!"

COACHING POINTS:
This drill can also be used effectively in tryouts for a team looking for
good-skating defensemen.

NAME OF DRILL: Defenseman's Breakout Drill
SKILL TO BE TAUGHT/ENHANCED: Defensemen Skills with
Breakouts; Support and Breakout Positioning for Forwards

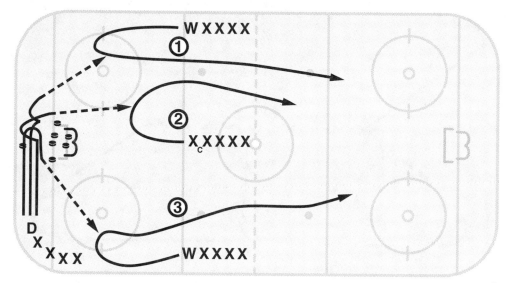

DESCRIPTION OF DRILL:
- Each defenseman becomes a very busy person in this drill as they will
  execute all three of the essential breakout passes to all three forwards.
- First of all, turn the nets around and place the pucks inside.
- On the whistle, the defenseman breaks from the corner, digs a puck out
  of the net and passes, first to the left wing, then to the center on the
  next whistle and then to his/her right wing on the third whistle.
- Each of the forwards will then break up ice for a shot on goal.

COACHING POINTS:
Be sure to work with the forwards on being in the proper spot for the
breakout.

NAME OF DRILL: Full-Speed Pivot Drill
SKILL TO BE TAUGHT/ENHANCED: Skating, Pivots, Defensemen Skills

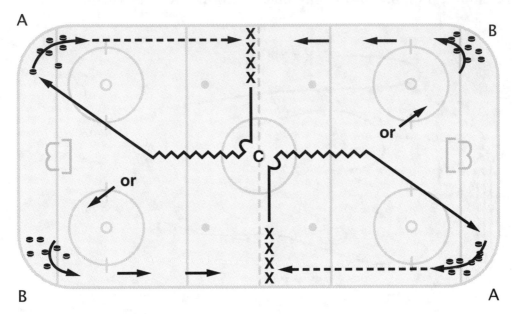

DESCRIPTION OF DRILL:
- Players line up along boards as shown. On the whistle, the first player breaks toward the coach located at center ice. He/she will pivot, at full speed, into a backskate mode. The coach will point to one corner or the other at which point the backskating player again pivots into a foreskating mode to puck up loose puck in the corner and outlet up the boards to the line of players he/she will be heading toward (Line A).
- Other variations of this drill include outlet passes flung around the boards to the other line (line B); also the coach can signal the backskate-to-foreskate pivot by dumping a puck into the corner.

COACHING POINTS:
- To facilitate the return of pucks to the corners, have the player on line who received the puck (outlet pass) simply return the puck back from whence it came.
- You may wish to have your defensemen work on their zone clears and a good way to do this is to tape a large "X" on the glass. Have the defensemen aim for this spot and clear the puck down the ice. Dartmouth assistant coach Rob Abel gave me this idea.

NAME OF DRILL: Defenseman's Puck Control
SKILL TO BE TAUGHT/ENHANCED: Backskating, Puck Control, Transition Passes

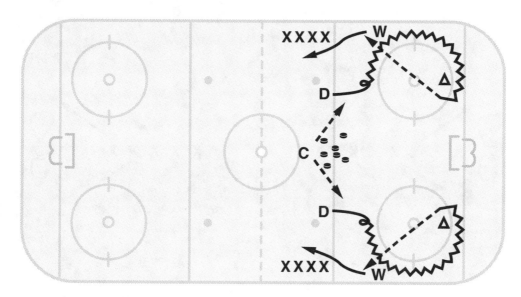

DESCRIPTION OF DRILL:
- Defensemen need to learn to control the puck effectively while backskating. This drill incorporates that as well as pivoting, opening to pass off and hitting the winger who has dropped back into a breakout/ support position.
- This drill can be worked on both sides of the ice simultaneously.
- The coach has a pile of pucks at the middle of the blue line and a line of defensemen nearby as shown.
- On the whistle, the defenseman takes three forward strides into the defensive zone, pivots to backskate and then receives a pass from the coach.
- The defenseman will carry the puck, backskating, around the base of the circle, pivot at the cone to face the supporting winger and pass off quickly.

COACHING POINTS:
- Speed is of the essence here; make this a hi-tempo drill.
- Have the defensemen accelerate in their backskating with cross-unders.
- Use your imagination for the wingers — once they get the puck, a 2-on-0 or a breakaway contest or a cone drill can be added to keep the drill functional for them.

NAME OF DRILL: Defenseman's Escape Drill
SKILL TO BE TAUGHT/ENHANCED: Eluding Checker in Tight Quarters

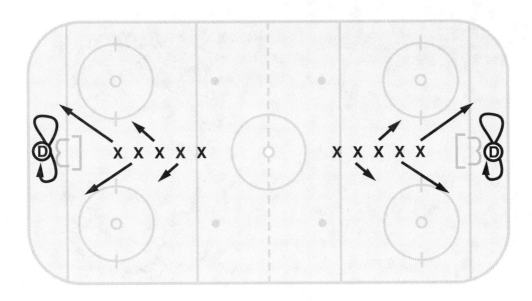

DESCRIPTION OF DRILL:
- Defensemen must be taught to escape a forechecker in their defensive zone and that is the purpose of this drill. It is important that they learn to tight-turn away from the checker rather than, as is typically done, try to stickhandle and deke, often to no avail.
- Line up a set of forechecking forwards as is shown. They will attack the defenseman from alternating sides and each on a whistle.
- The defenseman will use a series of tight-turn curls to retain control of the puck.
- Use both ends of the ice simultaneously.

COACHING POINTS:
- Note that the defenseman's pattern is basically that of a figure-8.
- Teach the defenseman to cross his hands over when tight-turning to the forehand side.
- Note that the defenseman always turns toward the boards.

NAME OF DRILL: Park Pass Breakout Drill
SKILL TO BE TAUGHT/ENHANCED: Defenseman's "First Pass" Skill

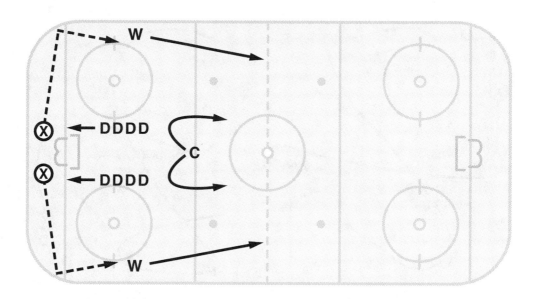

DESCRIPTION OF DRILL:
- Brad Park, the great former defenseman for the N.Y. Rangers and Boston Bruins, used to practice this pass. He aimed for the point on the boards at which the goalline met the boards. A pass hitting that precise spot will always rebound off the boards to a spot ideally located, as shown, for the breakout wing. Try it!
- Be advised that only left-handed shooters can work their way around the net to the left and righties to the right as shown since you must just clear the near post to fire the pass.

COACHING POINTS:
Not every rink is going to have boards as true and edges as clean as those that Brad Park played on. Those of us in the real world must test our corner boards. Often the receiving wingers will have to take the pass off their skates, but then this is a skill certainly worth developing, too.

NAME OF DRILL: Defenseman's Transition
SKILL TO BE TAUGHT/ENHANCED: Breakout Passing and Defending the 2-on-1

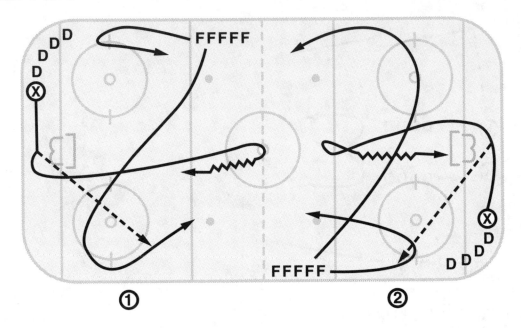

DESCRIPTION OF DRILL:
- Set your defensemen in the corners and forwards along the neutral zone boards as shown. Defensemen have pucks.
- Begin the drill with one end of the ice breaking out first (shown here as #1). The defenseman will carry from the corner to a breakout position behind the net. Setting up, he/she will then pass off to a forward stationed along the boards where they typically should be for breakout plays. This initiates a 2-on-0 up ice. The defenseman joins the rush only into the neutral zone.
- Once the breakout pass is launched at end #1, the players in end #2 will replicate the drill. The defenseman from end #1 picks up the two attackers from end #2 in a 2-on-1 scenario.

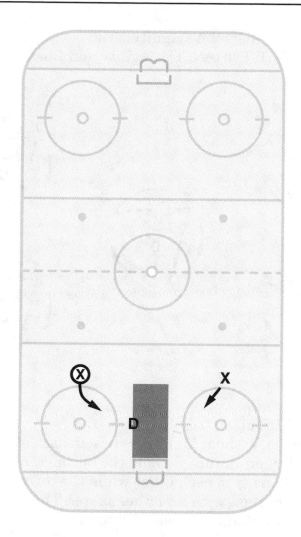

COACHING POINTS:
- Teach your defensemen to defend the "Defenseman's Alley" drawn here By holding position along the side of the alley nearest the puck-carrier they can "buy time" and not overcommit to the carrier, leaving the other attacker open for a pass.
- Shown here is a single defenseman holding his ground on the perimeter of the "alley."
- The "alley" is a conceptual line drawn from the goalposts to the top of the circles. Defensemen must control this area.

NAME OF DRILL: Defenseman's Agility Drill
SKILL TO BE TAUGHT/ENHANCED: Agility and Blocking the Centering Pass

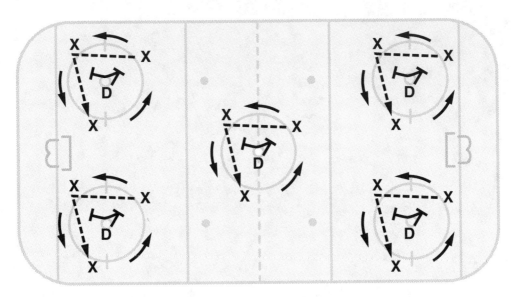

DESCRIPTION OF DRILL:
- Place a defenseman, without his or her stick, in each of the faceoff circles.
- Forwards are arrayed in threes along the perimeter of each circle.
- The forwards will pass to each other while the defender tries to block, stop, or deflect the pass with his or her skates. The forwards may skate along the perimeter and pass while in motion.

NAME OF DRILL: Defenseman's Control Drill
SKILL TO BE TAUGHT/ENHANCED: Skating, Pivots and Passing

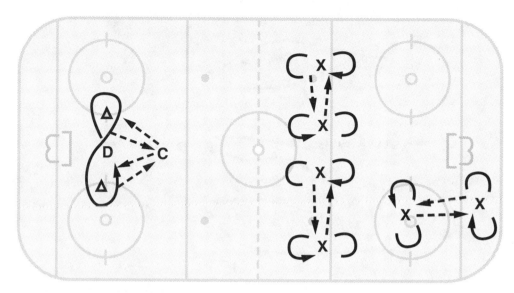

Phase I   **Phase II**

DESCRIPTION OF DRILL:
- Pair your defensemen at random all over the ice for phase II; put them with a coach at the hashmarks with cones for phase I.
- The first phase of this drill is done with one coach and two cones. Then remove the cones and the coach to allow the players to mirror the drill between themselves.
- PHASE I: Set the cones on the hashmarks and have the defenseman skate figure 8's between the cones, always facing the coach, pivoting the foreskate/backskate, and always keeping the stick on the ice. The coach will one-time passes to him.
- PHASE II: Remove the cones and simply have two defensemen mirroring each other in figure-8's to accomplish the same drill.

NAME OF DRILL: 3-1 Mini-Scrimmage
SKILL TO BE TAUGHT/ENHANCED: Evaluating Defensemen

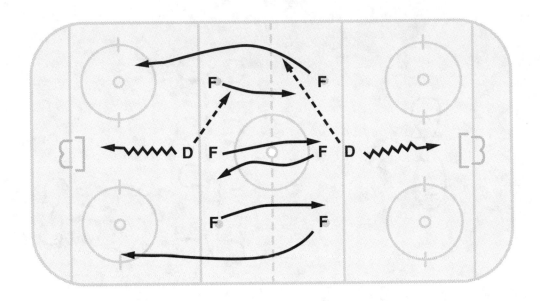

DESCRIPTION OF DRILL:
- Set three forwards and one defenseman along the blue lines as shown.
- The defenseman initiates the drill with a pass to one of the three forwards who will then attack the opposite direction. After the pass, the defender backskates to face a 3-man rush.
- The key here is to have the defenseman handle the puck so that coaches can evaluate his/her skills in escape and control. Do not allow them to simply knock the puck out of the zone to break up the rush.

COACHING POINTS:
Middle positioning is the key for the defenseman in this drill as they also learn to play the three-on-one.

NAME OF DRILL: Gainey's Angles Drill
SKILL TO BE TAUGHT/ENHANCED: Forwards Blocking Shots

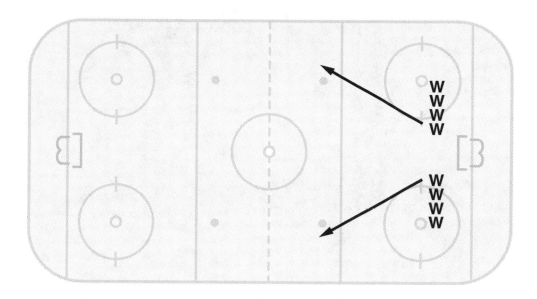

DESCRIPTION OF DRILL:

- Think about it: for forwards to go out and block point shots, they must know their angles out of the net every bit as well as the goalies must.
- Teach it by having them walk through it on the ice with pointmen at different locations along the blue line.
- While this is obviously a low-intensity drill, if indeed a drill at all, the time spent may provide dividends for more advanced teams.

COACHING POINTS:

This drill is named after the great defensive forward Bob Gainey. It was said that he knew his angles as well as any goaltender!

NAME OF DRILL: Point Puck Control
SKILL TO BE TAUGHT/ENHANCED: Defenseman's Point Play

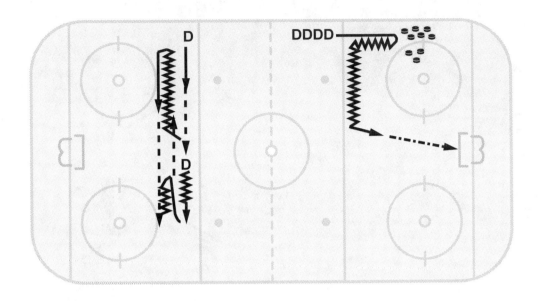

DESCRIPTION OF DRILL:

- In Zone 1, the defensemen are playing catch but with skating movement as they foreskate and backskate across the points. Coaches may elect to add the element of a fake shot or even drop one defenseman toward the circle as if they were utilizing the "umbrella" powerplay.
- Two drills are shown here. In Zone 2, the pointman pinches in for a loose puck, backskates to the points, slides across to the mid-point for a shot, squares with a pivot and blasts a shot on goal. (Coach my wish to add forwards down low to work on tip-ins).

NAME OF DRILL: Gap Control Drill
SKILL TO BE TAUGHT/ENHANCED: Teaching Defensemen to Close the
Gap Between an Enemy Forward and Himself

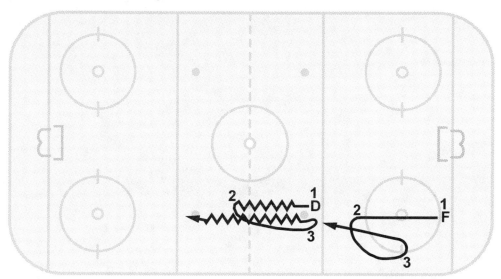

DESCRIPTION OF DRILL:
• Align one forward on a deep endzone dot and one defenseman on a
  neutral zone faceoff dot.
• Align one forward at the top of one of the deep endzone circles and set
  a defenseman facing him on a neutral zone dot as shown. Three whistles
  are involved in this drill; no pucks are needed unless you prefer to add
  the element of a 1-on-1.
• Basically, both players will mirror each other.
• Whistle #1: forward skates up ice while defenseman backskates.
• Whistle #2: forward (F) curls back to the hash while defenseman pivots
  into a foreskate to maintain the gap.
• Whistle #3: F turns and breaks forward while D pivots into a backskate.

COACHING POINTS:
When cycling up the boards and passing back into the corner, have the
player spin/pivot and face the boards for a crisp, hard pass.

GOALTENDER DRILLS

"The player who will make the most sacrifices will have as much a chance to reach the top as the one with the most talent."

Coach Clem Loughlin

NAME OF DRILL: Goalies: Punch-Outs and Kick-Outs
SKILL TO BE TAUGHT/ENHANCED: Goalie Deflecting Shots Into Corners

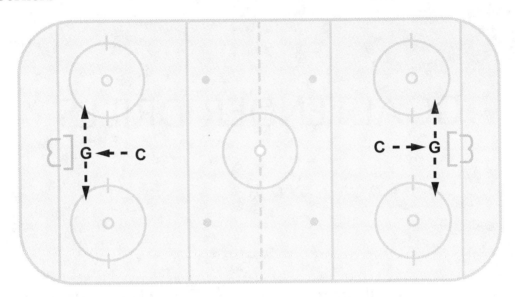

DESCRIPTION OF DRILL:
- Goalies need to be able to control rebounds by deflecting shots into the corners. This skill must be cultivated.
- Simply place a shooter near the circles and fire pucks, repeatedly, at their blocker. Keeping the blocker positioned in from their body and without a stick, they must "punch" the puck to the side.
- Repeat the drill with shots at their pads. Again, no stick is needed. The goalies must kick the shot into the corner.

COACHING POINTS:
- These drills can be done off-ice, too, especially the punch-out drill.
- If the coach is not an accurate shooter, simply throw pucks or balls at the goalie's blocker or pads.

NAME OF DRILL: Goaltender Agility Drills
SKILL TO BE TAUGHT/ENHANCED: Goalie Agility and Recovery

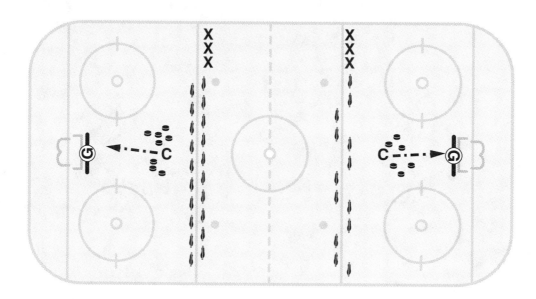

DESCRIPTION OF DRILL:

DRILL #1: BLUE LINE HOPS: Have goalies travel the length of the blue line hopping slowly and deliberately (i.e. — plyometrics call for a "loading up" concept of coiling before the leap) on one skate. Repeat twice on one skate and then execute twice on the other skate. Repeat sequence across the ice.

DRILL #2: BLUE LINE BABY STEPS: Have the goalies travel across the ice by taking short, choppy steps to quicken their feet and enhance agility.

DRILL #3: FLAT-BACK RECOVERY DRILL: Have the goalies in the nets lying flat on their backs. On a command they are to spring to their feet and face a coach/shooter.

• This drill can also be done with the goalies lying facedown on their stomachs.

COACHING POINTS:
• Drills #1 and #3 can be effectively performed off the ice, too.
• Drill #1 can also be done by hopping the goalie across the line on one skate.

NAME OF DRILL: Circle Shoot
SKILL TO BE TAUGHT/ENHANCED: Goaltender Reactions, Rebound Control

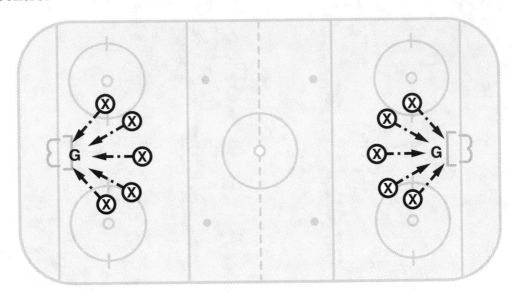

DESCRIPTION OF DRILL:
• Arrange 4-5 shooters in semicircular arch around goalie.
• Three drills emanate from this:
A. Coach calls each shot out loud by number, either randomly or sequentially; goalie must "square up" to each shot.
B. Rebound drill — one shooter fires at net and other pounces on rebound; goalie must control his rebounds and/or work to deflect it into corner out of the circle of shooters.
C. Post-to-Post-to-Slot — Have coach call out each shot; the shooters at either end of the circle will go first and alternate so until center shooter is up. Goalie must work on his square-up and his slide-n-glide post control.

- One teaching concept that can be imparted to your goalies is this modification of the "Popa System." Goalies can be taught their angles utilizing directional points on the ice. Then you can align shooters at each angle. This drill can be done off-ice, too, with a crease line painted on cement and cones set at the various points.
- Notice the numbers. Use them verbally as points of reference. Call them out as the shooters take their shots.

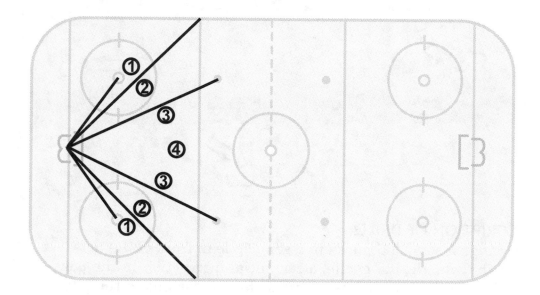

NAME OF DRILL: Poke-Check Drill (II): Goalies
SKILL TO BE TAUGHT/ENHANCED: Goaltender Poke-Checking Skills

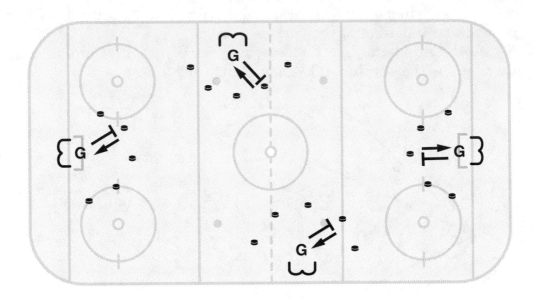

DESCRIPTION OF DRILL:
- Arrange a set of 3-5 pucks in a semicircle in front of the nets.
- On the whistle, the goalie, after initial instruction in the poke-check technique, is to attack from his or her crease out to the puck, poke-checking it away.
- After each puck is poked away, the goalie must return to the crease and attack another puck in sequence.

COACHING POINTS:
- Emphasize the leg-thrust along with the arm and stick thrust.
- Emphasize the slipping of the stick (i.e., "throwing" the blade of the stick out toward the puck) through the thrusting hand and grasping it only when the top-knob of the stick acts as a stopper.
- Emphasize quick recovery to face the next shooter.

NAME OF DRILL: 5-Circle Shuffle Drill (Goalies)
SKILL TO BE TAUGHT/ENHANCED: Stance and Set-Up Positioning for Goalies

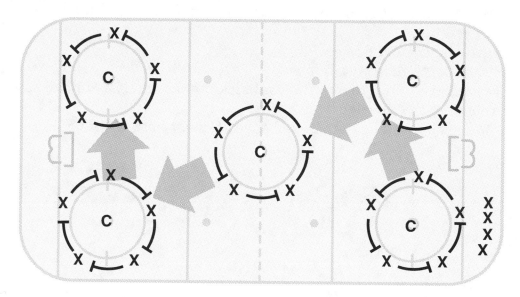

DESCRIPTION OF DRILL:
- Line the goalies in the corner of the rink and have them skate out to the nearest endzone circle.
- They will set up to face an imaginary shooter. All of the goalies should be standing on the edge of the circle facing inward to a coach.
- On each whistle they are to rotate in a given direction (be sure to work both directions!) and set up for the shot. They should set up about 4-6 times on each circle's perimeter.
- Emphasize the T-glide technique; watch for laziness as they will tire and tend to stand more upright as the drill progresses.

COACHING POINTS:
A good way to utilize full ice if you do not have a lot of goalies is to make this a two- or three-circle drill in one half, or third, of the ice while another set of goalies performs standard agility drills, explained on the following page, at the other end of the ice.

STANDARD AGILITY SEQUENCE FOR
GOALIES ON–ICE & OFF–ICE

Use hand or stick signals; use whistle and emphasize quickness.

1. Butterfly up-and-down.
2. Shuffle or T-glide post-to-post.
3. Tretiak (i.e., drop to on knee and kick other leg out as in pad save); repeat with other leg.
4. (On-ice only) Sliding stack-pad save. (Repeat both ways.)

NAME OF DRILL: Goalies: 3-Station Post Control
SKILL TO BE TAUGHT/ENHANCED: Goaltenders Hugging The Post

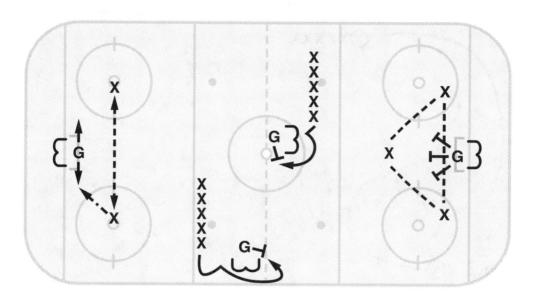

DESCRIPTION OF DRILL:
Several nets can be used if they are available.

ZONE A: Two shooters will pass the puck across the face of the goal as the goalie reacts by T-gliding from post to post. They will shoot when signaled by the coach.

ZONE B: Align the shooters to one side of the net. Upon command they will quickly carry behind the net and attempt to stuff the puck in near the opposite post as shown. Switch sides.

ZONE C: Align three shooters in a triangle in front of the net. They will pass the puck around quickly and randomly as the goalie reacts by setting up to face the shooter and shuffling to arrive in position.

NAME OF DRILL: Save-n-Stuff Drill: Goalies
SKILL TO BE TAUGHT/ENHANCED: Save Skills for Goalies

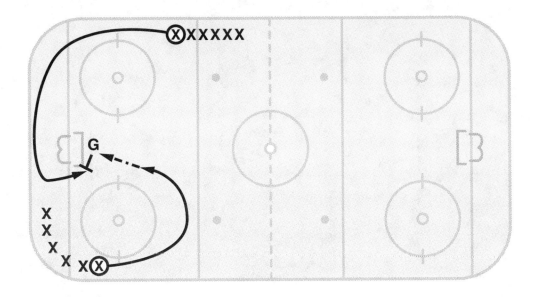

DESCRIPTION OF DRILL:
- Align players in corners and near blue line as shown.
- On the whistle a puck carrier from each line breaks toward the net as shown. The player in Line A will shoot first and the goalie, after having made the save against that shooter, must get to the far post to stop the second shot.
- This replicates a rebound which ends up on the stick of a post-hanging forward. The goalie must try to "stuff" the second shot by sliding across and preventing a rebound.
- Have the shooters switch lines after their shot.

NAME OF DRILL: Goaltenders Wall Drills
SKILL TO BE TAUGHT/ENHANCED: Reactions, Set-Ups, Quickness

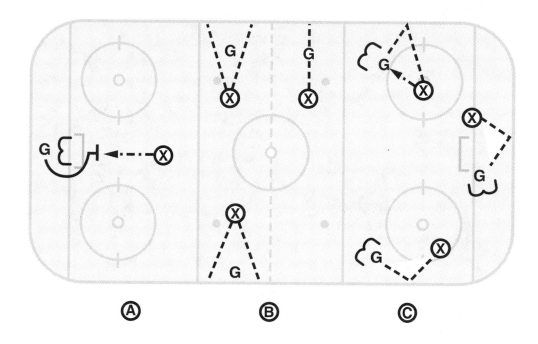

Ⓐ Ⓑ Ⓒ

DESCRIPTION OF DRILL:

Drill A: The goalie faces the boards behind the net. A shooter stands in front of the net. The shooter yells, "Now!" whereupon the goalie bursts, as quickly as possible, from behind the net to the front of the cage to face the shot. (The shooter must delay the shot somewhat, but the quicker the shot-release after the call of "Now!", the more the goalie has to work.)

Drill B: Using tennis balls, since they rebound better and can be "lifted" more easily by younger players, a shooter stands behind a goalie who is facing the wall about 5-10 feet away. The shooter fires the puck off the wall and the netminder must react with feet and gloves.

Drill C: Place a net along the boards, but at an angle. The goalie stands in and a shooter faces him or her. The puck can be shot directly at the net or off the wall and into the net. There is a good aspect to this drill which is not often worked. The goalie can "read" the stickblade of the shooter to determine where he/she intends to fire the puck.

NAME OF DRILL: Goaltender Stick Drills
SKILL TO BE TAUGHT/ENHANCED: Footwork, Agility and Set-Ups for Goalies

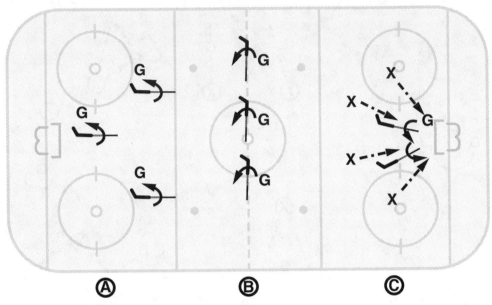

Ⓐ Ⓑ Ⓒ

DESCRIPTION OF DRILL:

Drill A: Goalies will place their sticks on the ice and leap over them in a side-hop format. After each leap, they must set up to face the shooter (imaginary).

Drill B: Goalies will place their sticks on the ice in front of them, leaping over in a forward hopping style, and again setting up to face the shooter.

Drill C: Goalies will place two sticks on the ice in front of the net in the positioning shown. There will be a set of live shooters, preferably four, in front of them. The goalie faces one shooter, leaps the stick in a side-hop, faces the next shooter, and so on. Live shots will be taken.

NAME OF DRILL: Deflection Boards
SKILL TO BE TAUGHT/ENHANCED: Screen and Angle Shots for Goaltenders

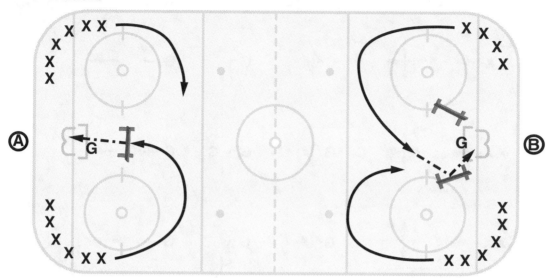

DESCRIPTION OF DRILL:

- Constructing a deflection board is simple. Use 4" x 4" lumber about 1-2' in length as the "legs" and use a piece of 4' x 8' (or smaller if need be) plywood as shown below:
- In Drill A, the shooter comes in and fires low-to-the-ice underneath the board so that the goalie must "get low" to read the shot, but more importantly, he/she will only be able to pick up the shot late so must react quickly.
- In Drill B, two deflection boards are set up at angles along the net as shown. The shooter skates in and can shoot directly on goal or off the board with a bank-shot that the goalie must react to.
- I have used smaller deflection boards for the deflection drill (B). These can be as compact as 2' x 8' (i.e. rip-cut a 4' x 8' sheet of plywood to create two boards. Realize that you will need the 4' x 8' board for the screen drill (A).
- I know of one coach who actually made a more portable screen-board by building a frame and draping a blanket over it.

NAME OF DRILL: 4-Station Agilities For Goalies
SKILL TO BE TAUGHT/ENHANCED: Agility Drills for Goalies

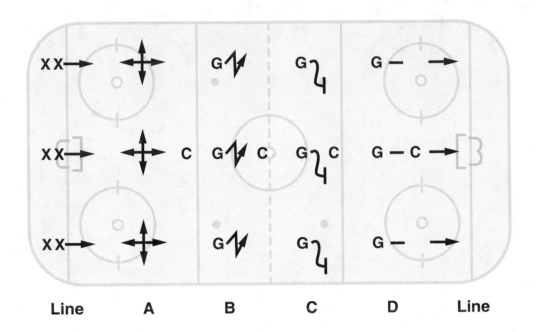

| Line | A | B | C | D | Line |

DESCRIPTION OF DRILL:
- Set a coach at the four drill stations as shown.
- Each drill station is one minute in duration with 10 seconds to move to the next drill area. The goalies will work their way up the ice in a linear fashion.
- Area A calls for the "Iron Cross" slide-n-glide in all four directions, each on the coach's command.
- Area B calls for up-down rapid-recovery drills on one knee and both knees, each on the coach's command.
- Area C calls for slide-and-stack as the goalies will slide into a stack-pad save to one side and then the other, each on the command of the coach.
- Area D is a prone recovery station as the goalies will lie down on their stomachs, backs or sides and recovery to their feet as quickly as possible, again on the coach's command.
- Note that this drill series utilizes the entire ice and goalies must have the ice all to themselves, hence it is best suited for goalie clinics, camps, or special goalie practices.

NAME OF DRILL: Screen Shots
SKILL TO BE TAUGHT/ENHANCED: Reactions, Playing The Shot
Through Screen

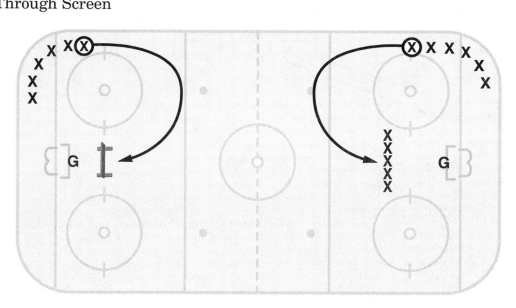

DESCRIPTION OF DRILL:
Set the goalies on their knees without sticks. Place a screen board in front of them or set a line of players as a screen. They must play the shot by finding the puck as quickly as possible.

NAME OF DRILL: Goalie Conditioning Drills
SKILL TO BE TAUGHT/ENHANCED: Leg Strength and Aerobic
Capacities

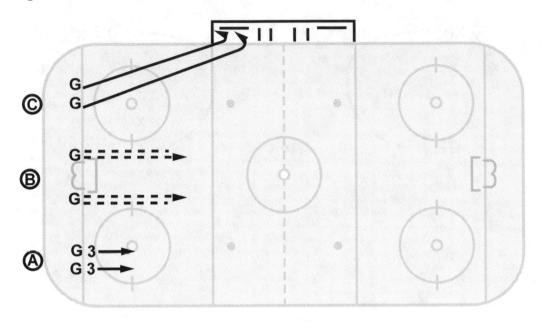

DESCRIPTION OF DRILL:
Four drills are described here and three are diagrammed.
A) Have the goalies push the nets the length of the ice; perhaps add a
   coach riding on the back of it.
B) Knee-walking: just as has been described in our off-ice work, have the
   goalies walk on their pads around the ice. This will tire, and hence
   strengthen, the thigh muscles (quadriceps).
C) Board Leaps: sprint to the bench and leap the boards just as if they
   were coming off the ice on a delayed penalty call.
D) The Weighted Hands: tape a flat 2 1/2-pound weight plate to the back
   of the blocker glove or the back of the wristguard on the catcher glove
   in practices. This will quicken their hands in games.

NAME OF DRILL: Goalie Clearing Drill
SKILL TO BE TAUGHT/ENHANCED: Goaltender Puck Control

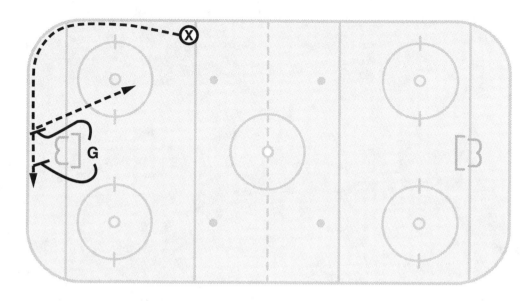

DESCRIPTION OF DRILL:
* Coach or player fires the puck around the boards and into the goalie's defensive zone.
* Goalie must read the puck's speed and skate around the net, to the proper side, to intercept it behind the net.
* The goalie will then work on his or her clearing the puck, up the boards or glass forehand and backhand.

POSITION–PLAY DRILLS
–Teaching Position Play

"A star can win any game; a team can win every game."

Coach Jack Ramsey

NAME OF DRILL: "Stay Within The Lines" Scrimmage
SKILL TO BE TAUGHT/ENHANCED: Teaching Position Play to
Beginners

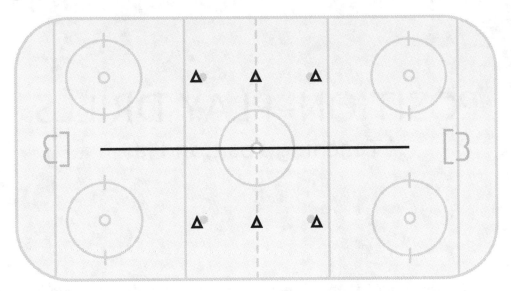

DESCRIPTION OF DRILL:

Teaching the concept of lanes can be a frustrating proposition for not only the coach but also the learner. The technique described here is not so much a drill but a teaching technique.

• Spray paint a line down the center of the ice between the hash marks. Tell your centers to stay with "reaching distance" of the line. More importantly, tell your defensemen and wings to remain on their side of the line, RW/RD and LW/LD.

• Set up three cones in the neutral zone on each side near the dots as shown. This will teach your wingers to stay wide in the middle ice section.

COACHING POINTS:

There will probably not be a need to employ both of these teaching techniques. Select one that works for you. You may raise some eyebrows if you spray paint on the ice, but rest assured that it scrapes right off when the Zamboni passes over it.

NAME OF DRILL: Tri-Scrimmage
SKILL TO BE TAUGHT/ENHANCED: Scrimmage, Line-Play

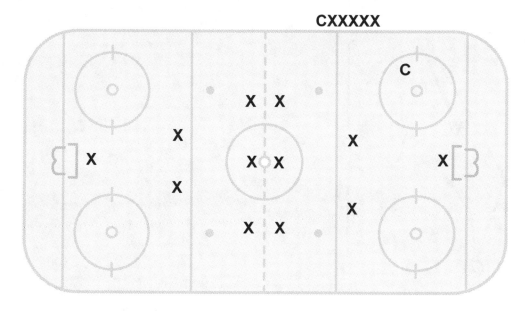

DESCRIPTION OF DRILL:
- Since most hockey teams have three full lines of five players, this is a good way to get the players working together amid an atmosphere of game situations and fun.
- Designate each line as a color (preferably have jerseys to match for each line) and send out two colors to play against each other. Coach them as to positioning with frequent whistles and stops (perhaps have an on-ice coach for each team so that individual mistakes can be addressed immediately).
- Since one line will be off the ice, assign a coach to work with them as they are on the bench. Rotate each line just as if they were skating a game shift. (Coaches often allow the players to remain out on the ice too long during scrimmages, so corrections are not made and weariness on the part of the players causes even more mistakes.)

COACHING POINTS:
Avoid the commonly used designations of A, B, or C or Line 1, 2, or 3 since these have qualitative connotations, and kids notice little messages like this.

NAME OF DRILL: 5-on-0 Passing Drill
SKILL TO BE TAUGHT/ENHANCED: Perimeter Passing, Power Play

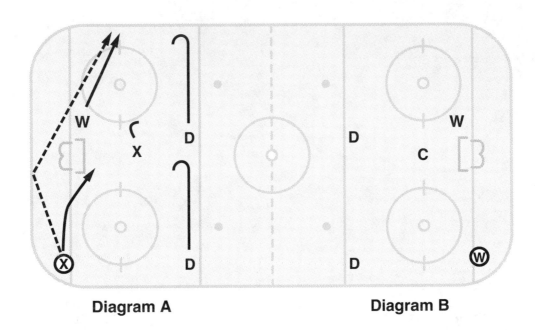

Diagram A   **Diagram B**

DESCRIPTION OF DRILL:
- To teach a team concept in 5-on-0 combinations, have your players line up as shown with wingers either in the corner with the puck or on the post, center in the slot and defensemen at the points.
- On the whistle, have the players execute sharp perimeter passes as well as the proper five-man "float" across the zone as the puck proceeds from one side to the other.
- Both ends of the ice can be worked at once to save time. In the diagrams above, Diagram A shows the proper float, and Diagram B shows the initial alignment.
- Once the players become proficient at the 5-0 passing, add in a penalty kill unit of four opponents, and even three opponents.

COACHING POINTS:
Players are never permitted to shoot until the coach blows a second whistle. The centerman should work on tip-ins and screens.

NAME OF DRILL: Breakout Skill Drill
SKILL TO BE TAUGHT/ENHANCED: Breakout Passes

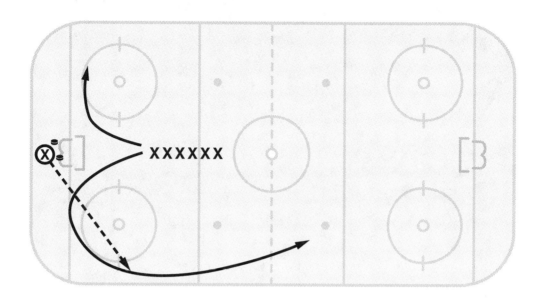

DESCRIPTION OF DRILL:
- Align forwards in the defensive slot area as shown and set a defenseman, with a puck, behind the cage.
- On the whistle, the lead forward in the line will break around the base of the faceoff circle, into the near corner and then up the boards to receive a breakout pass on the fly.
- The puck carrier can then proceed up ice for a breakaway shot on goal and a secondary drill (deke, board-pass, etc.).
- The next forward in line should break to the other side and the same defenseman should learn to outlet pass to that side, too, even if it means flinging a backhanded outlet along the boards.

NAME OF DRILL: Triangle Passing
SKILL TO BE TAUGHT/ENHANCED: Teaching the Offensive Triangle

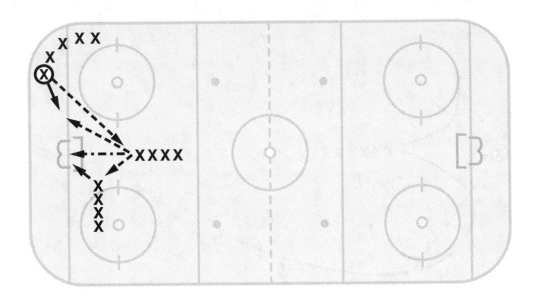

DESCRIPTION OF DRILL:
- This is a set-piece drill designed to teach the triangle concept of offensive zone play. It involves less than three passes and can be worked at higher speeds as players develop.
- Align one set of wingers along the boards leading into the corner.
- Align the other wings off the post and line the centers up in the high slot area.
- The wings in the corner will have the pucks and begin the drill.
- Passing sequences will call for a quick pass from the corner into the slot; a one-timed shot or pass to the post-wing will follow. The center may, if he/she chooses, tap-pass back to the corner wing who, after passing, broke for the near post.

COACHING POINTS:
Replicate the drill to the other corner and post.

NAME OF DRILL: 4-on-2 Half-Ice Drill
SKILL TO BE TAUGHT/ENHANCED: Offensive Skills and Finding the Open Man

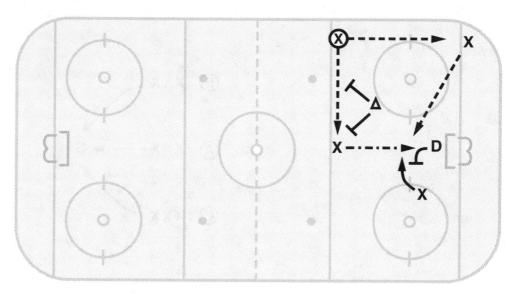

DESCRIPTION OF DRILL:

- Set four attackers and two defenders, the latter with the blades of the sticks in their hands, in one zone. Both ends of the ice can be used simultaneously.
- Tell the offensive people that two players will be open and it is their job to find them. Be creative on offense.
- The defenders are to hold down the fort as best they can, keeping one player high and one low. Have them try to anticipate passes and stick the puck away.

NAME OF DRILL: Close-In Triangle Drill
SKILL TO BE TAUGHT/ENHANCED: Working Puck Around in Tight Area,
Maintaining Offensive Triangle

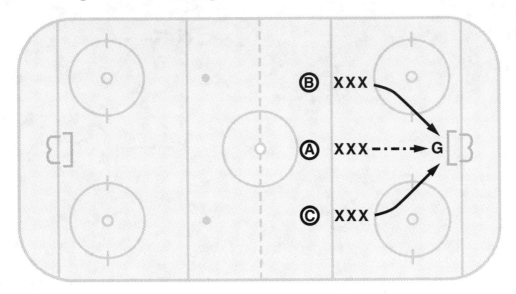

DESCRIPTION OF DRILL:
- Line A begins drill with shot on goal; a rebound should result.
- Lines A, B, and C will then chase-n-pass the puck around zone below the dots; take shot on goal.
- Lines of players need not clear the offensive zone as this adds to close-in quick-pass concepts.

COACHING POINTS:
- Lines B and C should drive hard for posts on initial shot.
- Attackers must make sure that slot and posts are covered.

NAME OF DRILL: UMass Boston's 3-on-3
SKILL TO BE TAUGHT/ENHANCED: Defensive Zone Coverage
DURATION OF DRILL: 30 seconds

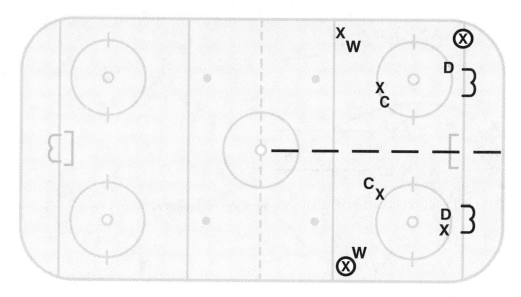

DESCRIPTION OF DRILL:
- Place two nets on goalline in areas shown above; defensive zone is now divided in half.
- Set a wing, center and defenseman in each half plus three attackers in control of the puck.
- Whistle to begin the 3-on-3; goalies are optional, but score is kept to add a competitive atmosphere.

COACHING POINTS:
- Depending upon your system, this 3-on-3 is excellent for having players learn/work their defensive zone coverages.
- You may wish to have the offense pass three times before shooting if your goalies are not present.

I would like to thank Paul Cannata, former coach at UMass Boston, for this drill.

NAME OF DRILL: 3-on-2 Breakout Drill
SKILL TO BE TAUGHT/ENHANCED: 3-2 Passing; 3-2 Defending

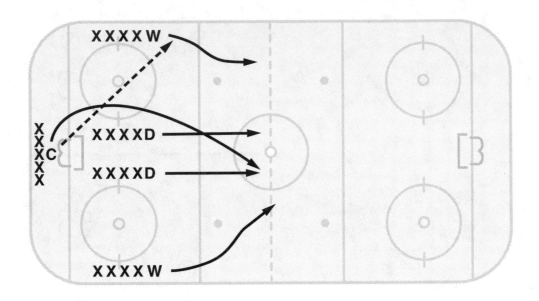

DESCRIPTION OF DRILL:
- Two defensemen align at hash marks (inside) and a centerman behind net.
- Centerman begins with breakout pass from behind net to wing along boards.
- Completing this drill can involve the entire attacking team driving to the other end of the rink in a 5-0 or the forwards curling back, once they reach the red line, to attack their own defensemen 3-2.
- This effectively creates a trailer play by having the centerman break out and enter the offensive zone late. Teach your players to look for this play as it creates excellent scoring opportunities.

NAME OF DRILL: Point Shots
SKILL TO BE TAUGHT/ENHANCED: Defenseman's Point Play

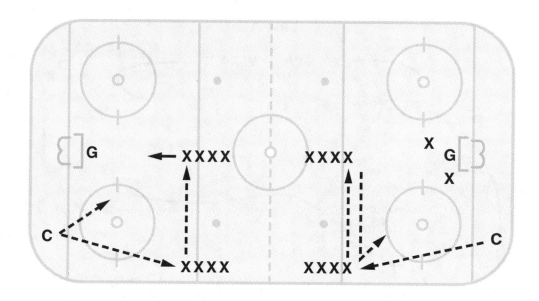

DESCRIPTION OF DRILL:
- Coach passes from corner to either pointman.
- Pointman either shoots or passes.
- Do not forget to work your forwards at the points since you may find yourself using them at that spot on the powerplay. Also, they may find themselves there after an offensive zone cycling sequence and they'd better have a sense of what to do.

COACHING POINTS:
- One-timed shots can be drilled if shooter's stick side is appropriate.
- Coach can add a screen and/or tip-in man to the drill.

NAME OF DRILL: Quick-Break Drill 1
SKILL TO BE TAUGHT/ENHANCED: Breakouts, Support, Passing, and Transition

Line A

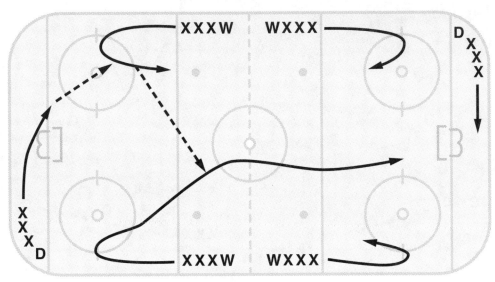

Line B

DESCRIPTION OF DRILL:
- Align defensemen in corner with pucks and forwards in neutral zone, as shown.
- On the whistle, the defenseman at one end carries behind his net and outlet passes to one of the wings who has curled back to his breakout position along the boards.
- In turn, the receiving winger will cross-ice pass to the other breaking wing. Note that this drill also teaches wings to look for the cross-ice wide wing who is often open against teams who play the neutral zone with less-than-perfect discipline.
- As soon as the wing in line A has passed off, replicate the drill at the other end of the ice.
- Defensemen can follow the play up ice, joining the rush in a 3-on-0, or they can play a 2-on-1 coming back at them.

NAME OF DRILL: Quick-Break 2
SKILL TO BE TAUGHT/ENHANCED: Breakouts, Transition

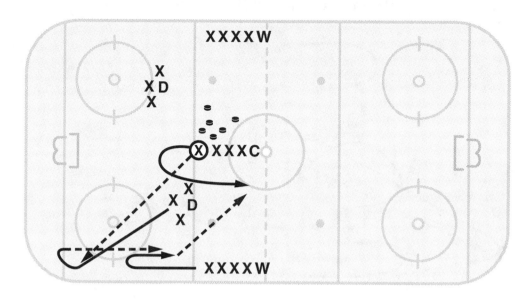

DESCRIPTION OF DRILL:
- Centermen line up on middle of blue line with pucks.
- Wingers line up along boards.
- Defensemen line up at top of circles.
- Center fires puck into corner and then hurries toward the winger for breakout pass. (A timing element may be necessary, so you may have to have the center count to three before curling; remember to have him/her curl toward the side of the winger receiving the first outlet pass — he/she reads this by reading the defenseman's turn toward his target.)
- The winger receives the outlet and passes quickly to the breaking center. The pass can be a touch-pass if the skill level warrants it. Also, if the players are advanced enough, have the winger receive the pass on the move as he/she breaks up the boards and the passing defenseman leads him/her.

COACHING POINTS:
Note how the defenseman can pick up the puck and turn to either side; the coach may wish to work particular defensemen on particular skills, depending upon individual weaknesses. A similar observation applies with a defenseman's skill on passing backhand or forehand. Work only one side of the ice at a time.

NAME OF DRILL: Breakout and 3-1
SKILL TO BE TAUGHT/ENHANCED: Breakouts, 3-1, Triangulation;
Coming Back Into Defensive Zone For Breakouts

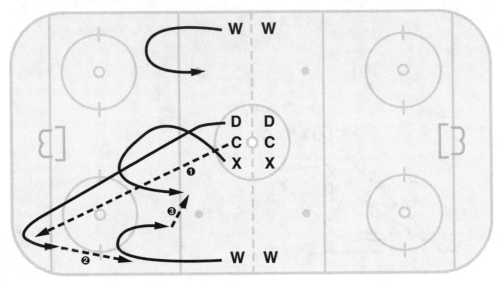

DESCRIPTION OF DRILL:
Pre-drill alignment is crucial here:
- Set two wings, two defensemen, two centers. Another set of two wings
  is designated spots along red line.
- Coach fires puck into a defensive zone, D picks it up and outlets to W or
  X on a breakout; the three forwards come back up ice 3-on-1 against
  the other D.
- After the shot or otherwise gaining control, D outlets to the second set
  of three forwards, and the drill is repeated.

COACHING POINTS:
- Make sure the forwards "buttonhook" back into the defensive zone rather
  than lazily hanging out at the blue line for breakout.
- Make sure that the forwards maintain their offensive zone triangle.

NAME OF DRILL: Breakout Bonanza Drill
SKILL TO BE TAUGHT/ENHANCED: Breakouts

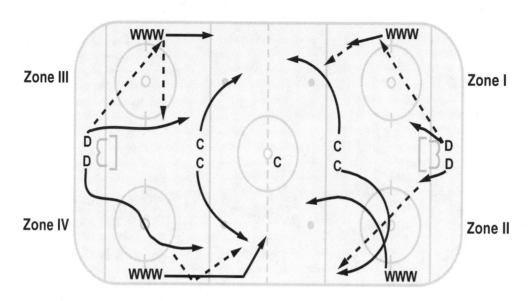

DESCRIPTION OF DRILL:

• This is simply a great drill for working on your team's breakouts.

• Four zones and four plays will be utilized. Set two defensemen behind each net and two centers on each blue line. All other wingers set up along the boards in their "post-up" position. Some coaches prefer their wingers even deeper, in a true post-up.

Zone 1 is a traditional triangular breakout but be sure to have the centerman break for the faceoff dot to keep the puck along the boards and out of the danger zone.

Zone II is a lane-change breakout wherein the center and wing switch assignments. This is good against wing-lock forechecking teams.

Zone III is used when the defenseman has time and space to skate the puck out of the zone and find his outlet in the neutral zone.

Zone IV calls for the execution of a give-n-go between the winger and the defenseman. This is good against teams who pinch their pointmen in.

• Coaches stand at center ice and direct traffic.

COACHING POINTS:

You can turn this into a 2-on-0 with the F dropping the puck back on a deep diagonal offensive zone tactical pass or you can make it a 1-on-1 with another D, on the line indicated, playing the attacker 1-on-1.

CONDITIONING DRILLS
— Pre- and Post-Practice
— Pre-Game

"A good coach will make his players see what they can become rather than what they are."

Coach Ara Parseghian

NAME OF DRILL: Pre-Practice Warm-Ups
SKILL TO BE TAUGHT/ENHANCED: Stretching and Skating Agility and Balance
DURATION OF DRILL: 5-10 minutes

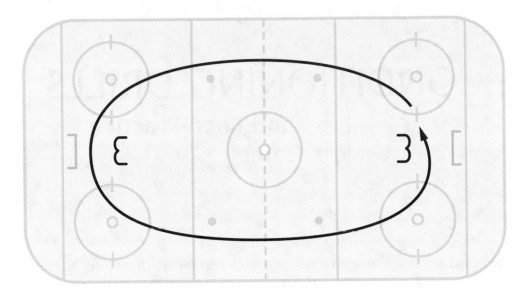

DESCRIPTION OF DRILL:
Move nets in so that they are set on the hash marks. Have players skate laps around rink/nets. In between blue lines, a different stretching drill is demonstrated and executed.

Stretching Drills:
- Back-arches (2 hands on stick overhead and arch back).
- Toe-touches.
- Sit down on "haunches" and glide (a.k.a. Russian Dancer).
- Toe kicks: holding stick at arms' length in front, have skaters balance on one skate and kick end of stick w/other skate (can add cross-over and kick).
- In-out skating pattern (keep skates on ice and alternately spread legs/ pull together).
- Sit down while skating and grab heels.
- Standard groin stretch (can be done w/stick overhead, too).
- Knee lift: pull knee upwards with stick.
- Twists: stick behind lower back, wide base to skates — twist; stick resting on shoulders, wide base, bend over — twist.

- Airplane spins: stick held w/both hands shoulder width, alternately twist in front (a.k.a. "air guitar") stick held in one hand at midpoint — twist.
- Knee drop (touch knee to ice and recover; hold for 3-4 seconds).
- Hammer-downs: 2 hands on end of stick, wide foot-base and touch ice with hands and stick.

COACHING POINT:

If you are skating the players in one circular direction for your stretching, warm-ups, skate them in the other direction for an ensuing agility phase.

NAME OF DRILL: Advanced Individual Warm-Ups
SKILL TO BE TAUGHT/ENHANCED: Stretches

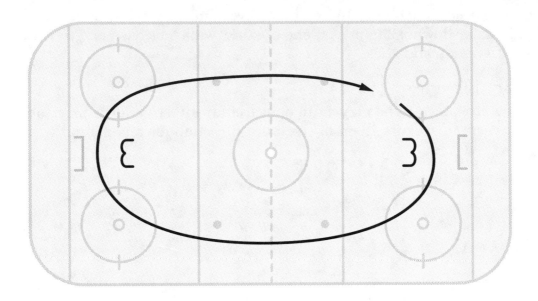

DESCRIPTION OF DRILL:
As the players circle the ice prior to beginning a practice, there are the conventional stretches discussed earlier in this volume. Here are some more advanced ones.
• Skate with both hands on the stick, but behind the skates and crouched over.
• Leg kicks, but swing the leg back fully and then forward as high as possible and then out to the side all with a relatively stiff knee.
• Pull one ankle upward with the hand, just as sprinters and runners often do, but we perform this drill on one skate.

COACHING POINTS:
• As can be seen, these drills also call for elements of balance and body control.
• Also, I prefer to place the nets on the hashmarks, as shown, for all of my pre-practice warm-ups to prevent traffic jams behind the cages.

NAME OF DRILL: Conditioning 1: Positional Windsprints
SKILL TO BE TAUGHT/ENHANCED: Conditioning, Speed, Concept of "Lanes"

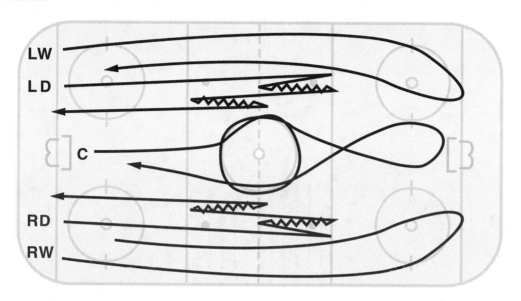

DESCRIPTION OF DRILL:
- Form players into positional lines, as shown, for centers, wings, and defensemen (D).
- On whistle, sprint in lanes shown and return to line.

COACHING POINTS:
- Defenseman uses backskating when wavy lines are indicated.
- Center will cross-over accelerate around neutral zone circle in one direction on way down the rink and reverse direction when returning.
- Wing will jam to full stop, tap post with stick, cross-over jump-start accelerate to return up ice.
- Goalies can sprint from the crease and leap over the boards into the bench area (not shown).

NAME OF DRILL: Conditioning 2: Board Jumps
SKILL TO BE TAUGHT/ENHANCED: Conditioning, Line Changes

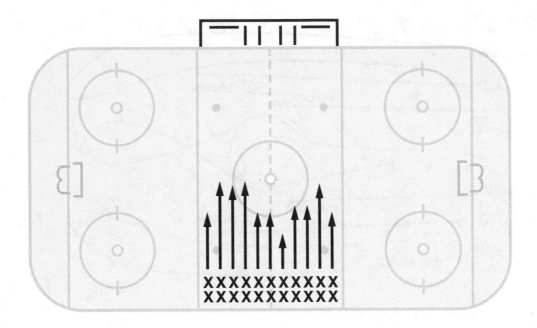

DESCRIPTION OF DRILL:
- Try board jumps for conditioning or for "getting your team's attention."
- Simply line them up along the boards in the neutral zone and opposite the players' benches. On the whistle, send all forwards sprinting across the ice; they hop on to the bench, back off and return to the starting point. Then send the defense, including the goalies back and forth.
- The board jumps can be grueling.

NAME OF DRILL: Conditioning Drill 3: Suicides
SKILL TO BE TAUGHT/ENHANCED: Stamina

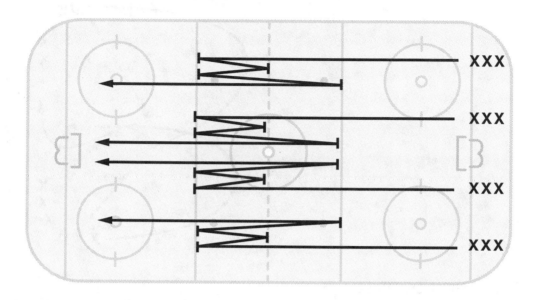

DESCRIPTION OF DRILL:
- A drill taken from basketball coaches is most certainly applicable in our sport.
- Lining the players up along one endzone goalline and having them spring to a far blue line, for instance, returning to the near blue line and then all the way down the ice is but one pattern to this infamous conditioning drill.
- Imaginative coaches out to send a message to their players might add the red line to the schemata.
- Insist that all stops be facing one side of the rink to ensure stopping abilities on either edge of the skates. Also insist that these sprints be done all out.
- Durations of 45 seconds followed by 15 seconds of rest, or 60 seconds followed by 20 seconds of rest or 70-20 and so on can reflect not only conditioning elements but also the coach's mood and/or his appraisal of the team's work ethic in the previous game.
- Other skating configurations include side-to-side sprints or figure-8's in the endzone thirds, etc.

NAME OF DRILL: Traditional Pre-Game Warm-Ups

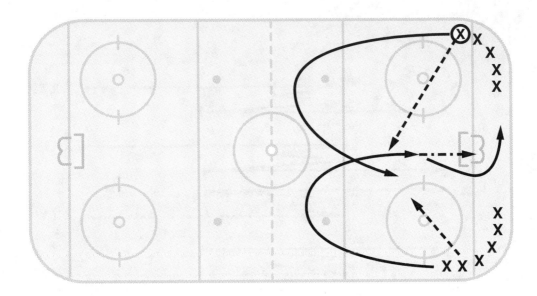

DESCRIPTION OF DRILL:
- Players line up in each corner and each side has pucks.
- One player breaks from his or her corner, around the neutral zone faceoff dot and into the attacking zone whereupon he/she receives a pass from the other line. They skate in for a shot on goal.
- Once the pass is released, the passer replicates the skating pattern to the mirror side, breaking immediately after launching the pass.
- Players should switch lines after each skate-in.

COACHING POINTS:
Tell your players that since this drill is designed to warm up the goalies as much as the skaters, no slapshots should be taken (this avoids potential injury) and no dekes should be employed. Have the shooters work the goalie's feet and gloves.

NAME OF DRILL: Pre-Game Warm-Up Variation
SKILL TO BE TAUGHT/ENHANCED: Passing/Shooting

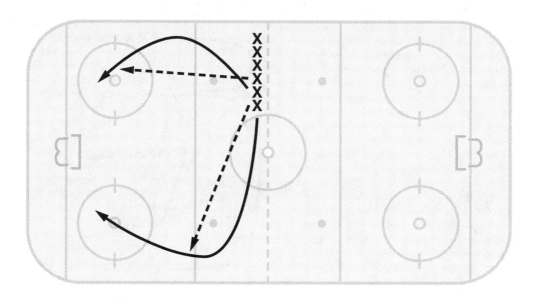

DESCRIPTION OF DRILL:

- After warm-up shots have been taken at blue line, drop same line of players back to red line. First player breaks wide and into zone; second player passes to him; that player then breaks into zone and third player passes to him.
- A variation off this can be facilitated by having first pass completed and then two players breaking into zone would pass between themselves.

NAME OF DRILL: Pro Pre-Game Drill
SKILL TO BE TAUGHT/ENHANCED: Passing; 2-L's

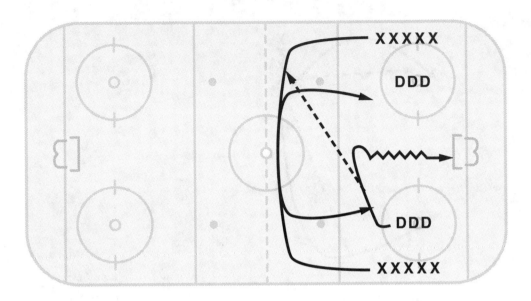

DESCRIPTION OF DRILL:
This is a drill used by many professional teams as part of their pre-game warm-ups. I have seen it used by the New Jersey Devils and the Hershey Bears myself. It plays out as follows:
- Align defensemen just outside the endzone faceoff dots and the forwards along the boards as shown.
- To begin the drill, a defenseman will pass to a forward who is criss-crossing with the other forward in the neutral zone just across the blue line.
- After passing, the defenseman breaks forward and then pivots into a backskating mode to confront the approaching 2-on-1.
- As soon as the shot is taken, the other side's defenseman initiates a replication of the drill. Note that the forwards have alternated lines after taking the shot.

NAME OF DRILL: Sorrentino Pre-Practice
SKILL TO BE TAUGHT/ENHANCED: Skating and Shooting; Goalies'
Reactions

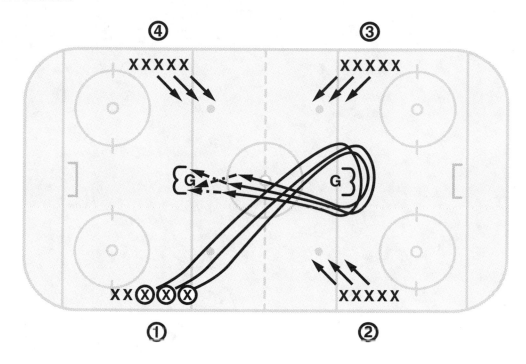

DESCRIPTION OF DRILL:
• Align four sets of players just outside the neutral zone, as shown. Number each for command purposes.
• The first three in each line (each must have a puck) will break out at high speed across the neutral zone, around the net and attack the other net shooting in rapid fire.
• The goalies must react to shots.

COACHING POINTS:
Lou Sorrentino coaches the Brick Hockey Club in Central New Jersey. He notes that he likes to begin practices with this drill.

OFF-ICE DRILLS

"A smart coach will watch for something he doesn't want to see and listen to what he doesn't want to hear."

Coach John Madden

I have long held the firm belief that much of what is taught in the game of ice hockey can be learned off the ice. The obvious exception is skating itself, but even that is less difficult than it used to be with the advent of in-line roller skates. Unless a coach has unlimited access to a rink for his or her team, he or she is remiss in not including off-ice training. Of course the weather must be factored in, but in the more northerly climates you can have all of the ice you want. I teach and coach in New Jersey; we may have limited ice-time, but we have mild enough winters to offer us excellent opportunities for off-ice work.

Drill #1 Positional Work: Use a parking lot and some street hockey goals to teach faceoffs, breakouts, offensive play patterns and so forth. These can be taught on foot or on in-line skates. I have even used our high school football field, having the players pass a rubber ball in lieu of a puck as they run through the patterns.

Drill #2 Faceoffs: There is no need at all to have your centers work their faceoff techniques on the ice. This wastes valuable skating time. Have them report for "Faceoff Practice" with only their gloves and sticks.

Drill #3 Shooting: Cut plexiglass, plastic, or formica boards to sizes in the neighborhood of 3' x 3'. Check with the rink your team skates in since they often have old sections of the glass and boards they are discarding. Use real pucks and work on all of your shots — slap, snap, wrist, and backhand — against nets, target nets, target boards or even through tires. By the way, as a coach who is always cost-conscious, why not make your own nets from wood, PVC pipe or scrap metal?

Shooting Drill 3.1: Use "Shooter Tutor" canvas net covers or home-made shooting boards made of plywood, canvas, or plexiglass/plastic. Each of these target boards has the five 'holes' where shooters want to aim their shots against a goalie. Each board or canvas must be 4' x 6'. And you need to be able to fasten these against the mouth of the goal with hooks or tie-ons. Shoot backhand and forehand.

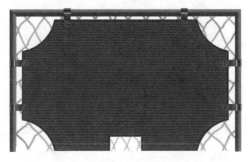

Shooting Drill 3.2: Use the tire in the shooting drills in Volume I to work backhand or forehand snap shots.

Shooting Drill 3.3: The Fallen Goalie Drill. Place a 12-15" board in an upright position by fastening a perpendicular stabilizing board along the bottom. You will need a plastic shooting board abutted right up along side the "fallen goalie" (i.e. — the upright board laying across the mouth of the goal). Work the flip shot over the fallen goalie with backhand and forehand shots.

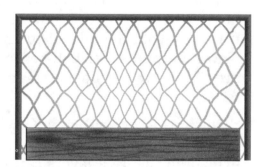

Shooting Drill 3.4: Backhand Target Boards. Paint round targets on plywood boards of any substantial size (3' - 4' x 4' - 6'). You may wish to number them with point totals to make your shooting games competitive. Use plywood with backhand shots to minimize wear and tear on the board.

Shooting Drill 3.5: Tip-ins. When your players are involved in forehand shooting, place two additional players on each side of the target in order to work on their tip-ins.

Shooting Drill 3.6: Contests. Players love competition. When you are working against a Shooter Tutor assign a point value to each hole (e.g. — three for the upper corners, one for the lower corners and two for the five hole). Backhands can be incorporated, too. (Note: I have been using the name "Shooter Tutor." This is actually a trademark item; other types of target boards exist, but the Shooter Tutor is one that is well-designed and of excellent quality.)

Drill #4 Stickhandling: Just about everything you do on the ice can be drilled off the ice in stickhandling, too. Utilize your traditional cone drills, 1-on-1, 2-on-0, etc. Two things to consider, however, include whether or not you want your players on roller blades for these drills and what type of puck or ball should they use. Generally speaking, the younger and less-skilled the player, the more they should learn on foot. This way, they will be able to concentrate on the stickhandling tasks. As for the ball or puck medium, consider the surface you are working on first. Plastic pucks are excellent and obviously more realistic, but they bounce and roll or rough surfaces (they are best used on gym floors). Street hockey balls are fine for the rough surfaces, but be aware of the fact that they come in warm weather or cold weather styles, indoor or outdoor. The "deader" the ball, the better it is since the bounce factor will be reduced. Tennis balls are often used by kids in the streets. But they bounce and roll too much for teaching and drill purposes. New-style pucks with ball-bearings seem interestingly hi-tech, but they are expensive and do not work that well on rough or semi-rough surfaces.

Stickhandling Drill 4.1: Knock-Downs. Airborne puck control is certainly a valuable skill, however, it need not be learned, practiced and drilled on the ice. Players can flip pucks or balls over to a teammate spaced 12-15 feet away. The receiver "traps" the puck/ball. This can be done in stationary or moving drills performed off the ice.

Stickhandling Drill 4.2: Quick-Hands. Have the players enhance the quickness of their hands in stickhandling by using golf balls (this is effectively done on the ice, too!). An additional skill enhanced by using golf balls is "widening the stickhandling range." Since players all too often fall into a "comfort zone" of stickhandling width which should be widened until their arms and stick is held at fully-outstretched distances (up to 12' for mature players!), golf balls more easily teach this.

Stickhandling Drill 4.3: Tip Control. Enhance stickhandling skills by using tennis or street hockey balls and have the players dribble a figure-8 pattern between their gloves. Start slowly and increase the tempo. (G=gloves)

Stickhandling Drill 4.4: Eye/Hand Coordination and Airborne Puck Control. Use tennis balls for this drill since they offer the best rebounding capabilities. Have the players dribble the ball by bouncing it, basketball-style, with their sticks downward against the ground surface. Then they will control it in the air by bouncing the ball upward off their stick. Perform these drills in sets of 10 repetitions each.

Stickhandling Drill 4.5: One-Hand Control Drills. An often overlooked component of stickhandling is the need to control the puck with one hand, usually to escape a check or power-deke around a defender. Utilizing cones and imagination, the coach can drill his or her players in their use of one-hand on the stick. Have them control the puck or ball with one hand to draw across their body or cup the puck around a cone as they sweep outside and around an imaginary defender. The "slip-through" move can be worked in this drill, too.

THE WHIFFLE–PUCK

This little gimmick is going to be patented soon by someone out there, but here is how one is made at home.

Take a common whiffleball and a tennis ball. Cut the tennis ball in half. Then halve it again and yet again. You should cut it into eight slivers much like one would cut an orange into slices.

Now stuff the tennis ball "peels" into the whiffleball holes. The result is a weighted whiffleball which glides rather than bounces, feels like a puck and stickhandles, as well as passes, like a dream.

It's worth making several of these for your players. Then apply the stickhandling and passing drills we outlined earlier. Do not use these for shooting.

I'd like to recognize Red Gendron, assistant coach for the New Jersey Devils, who presented the idea in a coaches clinic.

SOME DRILLS WITH WHIFFLE–PUCKS

Use the quick-hands drill described in the segment on stickhandling. Set cones about 4' apart and have the players straddle them as they weave the whiffle-pucks through the cones.

Also set cones about 8' apart as markers and have the players strive to widen their "comfort zone" of stickhandling width by going down the middle of the cone set, but reaching out toward each cone.

The gloves-off figure-8 drill described earlier is excellent here, too.

Realize that the whiffle-puck is heavier and less "bouncy" so you may prefer tennis balls and street hockey balls/pucks when shooting on goalies.

Drill #5: Stride Training: There is an element of skating which can be drilled outside and that relates to knee flexion, stride, thrust, hip flexion and power. In other words, the legs can be strengthened for powerskating in off-ice training.

Powerskating Drill 5.1: Linear Plyometric Bounding. While I hesitate to incorporate full-scale Plyometric routines (out of concern for knee stress), there is a drill which is of definite benefit when properly executed. Lay out a marked course about 20' - 30' in length. Have your players stride out at a 45-degree angle gaining ground in terms of distance and width. Of course, they should use alternate strides and seek to flex the knee at a 90-degree bend. Some cautionary words here: be sure to perform this and any other plyometrics you choose to do on soft surfaces such as grass fields. Never do "plyos" on concrete or macadam. Secondly, instruct your players to work this drill slowly and deliberately rather than hurriedly skipping through it. Teach them to "load up" with proper knee and hip flexion before exploding into the thrust. If your players complain of knee stress after doing this drill, listen to them.

Stride sequence: (one leg at a time, as if skating in slow-motion)

```
L L L L L L L
 \/ \/ \/ \/ \/ \/ \  ————————▷
  R R R R R R
```

The thrust should come from the leg which is under the body's center of gravity; this is a basic concept in all successful powerskating.

Powerskating Drill 5.2: Glide Boards. Plastic topped boards can be purchased from manufacturers, but they can also be homemade with formica-top boards or even old sections of rink boards if they are plastic coated. Fasten a 2" x 4" board about 2' in length at the ends of the glide surface. This serves as a safety/control edge so the skater does not fly off the ends of the glideboard. Use old hockey sox cut in half as "booties" which the players slip over their sneakers or shoes to enhance the glide capabilities and minimize time wastage involved in taking off their shoes. The blocking boards would be placed at any-where between 4' and 6 1/2' apart, depending upon the age and height of your trainees. A handy formula is that the distance apart should equate with their body's height. In training, have the players glide, one leg at a time, side to side along the board's surface. They should emphasize the push factor as well as knee and hip flexion. Have the players work to keep their center of gravity low; they will want to straighten up. Employ a timing element in their training. Begin with 20-30 seconds in three sets as a routine and increase the timing up to two minutes or more. Performed well, their thighs will be screaming!

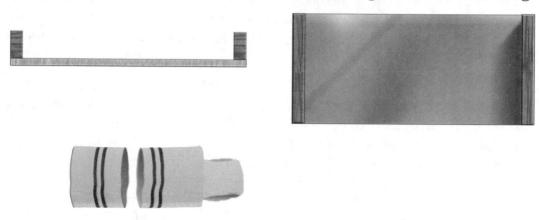

Powerskating Drill 5.3: In-Line Skates. In-line skates have come into such wide acceptance that entire teams mandate that their play-ers keep these skates in their equipment bags! Virtually every aspect of skating, except the hockey stop, can be practiced and drilled. In ad-dition, stickhandling, shooting, passing, team play and so forth all can be effectively worked off the ice just as they would be on the ice. How-ever, there are two further training components which can be addressed with in-line skates: conditioning and leg strength development. Six weeks before the start of the season, have your players begin a specific training program utilizing roller blades. As they would with a running program, set time or distances for each workout beginning lightly and increasing for distances of up to four miles by week six. You will find that not only is their wind/aerobic capacity up to satisfactory levels, but their leg strength has been increased, too. Monitor players with knee injuries. I have known some players to complain of aggravation while others feel that in-line skates stress their knees less than dis-tance running will. It seems to be an individual thing, so keep a close record on this regard. As an ancillary note, I recently had one player who played baseball as well as hockey for me and we discovered, to our delight and surprise, that the player's timed run to first base had improved by 1.3 seconds over the course of one year. Knowing that he did little else than in-line skate, we can surmise that in-line skating may help in terms of speed enhancement akin to the old theory of overload with ankle weights. (I heard of one college team that requires eight miles of in-line skating four times per week during the summer months!)

Drill #6: Goaltenders' Off-Ice Work: Goalies can benefit from off-ice training as well. The glide boards, stickhandling drills, and even shooting can help them in their unique skill requirements. However, there are some additional and specialized drills which can be employed off the ice for netminders.

Goalie Drill 6.1: Tennis Ball Shots. Professional goaltender Glenn "Chico" Resch used to face shots from a tennis ball shooting machine during the off-season to hone his skills. Even on the amateur level, young shooters can propel a tennis ball with amazing velocity. A goalie facing a bevy of shooters blasting tennis balls at him or her can certainly sharpen reaction-time, especially if the shots are directed at given problem areas such as feet or high stick-side. Tennis balls are preferred not only because of the speed factor, but also because they hurt less when they hit an unprotected area on the goalie, the feet and ankles for instance.

Goalie Drill 6.2: The Puck Catch. Have young goalies play the traditional game of catch with a real puck and using their catcher gloves. Coaching point — have them fling the puck in a sidearm manner, even frisbee style so that it spins horizontally rather than tumbles. Obviously, the flat-spin flight-path more closely replicates an actual shot.

Goalie Drill 6.3: Rebound Control. Have the goalies stand either in net or against a wall. Throw or shoot tennis balls or street hockey balls at their blocker and/or leg pads specifying that they are to deflect the ball to the corner. This skill is easily transferable to the ice.

Goalie Drill 6.4: Eye-Hand Coordination Wall Drills. In this sequence of drills, line your goalies up against a wall with a rubber ball in their left hand. They are to use the shuffle and sidestep technique that they would use in game conditions as they bounce the ball of the wall, throwing and catching the ball in their left hand. Repeat the drill returning along the wall in the opposite direction utilizing the right hand. Then repeat the shuffle, emphasizing they are to flex at the knees and hips (since they will want to straighten up as fatigue sets in), but using both hands and two balls simultaneously. The latter portion of this drill enhances peripheral vision.

Goalie Drill 6.5: Leg Strengthening. Have the goalies "walk" on their knees for moderate distances, perhaps 50 yards. Of course they should have their plastic street hockey leg pads on. Any time that the goalies will be asked to drop to their knees in drills or in stopping shots, they should be using plastic pads since their leather goalie pads will suffer damaging wear-and-tear. The purpose of this drill, however, is to strengthen the thigh muscles employed in lugging about their on-ice leather leg pads. Another good leg-strengthening drill is called "Frog Leaps" and it calls for the goalies to squat down low on their haunches and leap upward in quick, powerful thrust upon the coach's command. The "Frog Kicks" are done without leg pads and I have my entire team do them as part of a regular plyometric program.

Goalie Drill 6.6: Reaction Drills. Have the goalie face a wall about 6' away. From behind him or her, the coach throws a rubber tennis ball against the wall. The goalie will have to react to this rebounding ball very quickly to stop it. The thrower/coach should vary both the height and width to create different rebound angles for the goalie to contend with. Coaches can also ask their goalies to spring upward from butterfly positions or lying prone on their backs or from their knees to upright recovery stances.

Goalie Drill 6.7: Quick-Feet Wall Soccer. Give each goalie a soccer ball and have them stand against a wall, facing it from some 5 — 10 feet away. By kicking the ball low and to their sides, they can enhance their footwork.

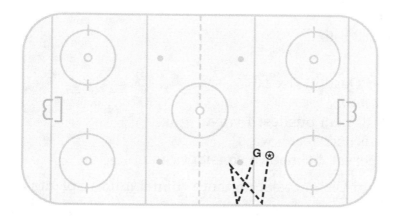

The better they become at this drill, the closer they can move to the wall.

Goalie Drill 6.8: Our goalies utilize the Popa system involving a "horseshoe" concept. We have the crease and the horseshoe spray painted on a macadam area outside our school. By calling out numbers at random, we can have our goalies shift to the proper location to face imaginary shots along the horseshoe.

Drill #7: Conditioning: Most coaches have their own thoughts about conditioning their athletes, but here are a few suggestions about aerobic conditioning and weight training which I have excerpted from my high school team's playbook.

AN ICE HOCKEY WEIGHT TRAINING PROGRAM
In season: twice per week; out-of season: three times per week

Remember, in ice hockey, it is the lower body which counts. Forget single-rep maximums on the bench press and curls for the beach!

LEGS:
Squats/Hip Sled/Leg Press 3 x 10
(choose one)
Leg Extensions 3 x 10
Lunges 2 x 10 each way. Need to work in three directions:
A. Feet planted and sway side-to-side
B. Stride forward (rear knee touches ground)
C. Stride out at 45-degree angle with each leg

UPPER BODY:
Bench Press 3 x 10
Standing Dumbell Flys 2 x 10
Seated Press 2 x 10
Curls 3 x 10
Wrist Roller 2 sets

BACK:
Stiff-Legged Deadlift 3 x 10
Sit-Ups 1 x max
Neck Work (2-man pushes; 4-ways)
1 set of 10 seconds (each way)
You can superset if time is a consideration.

Conditioning: Distances of no more than 2 miles. Sprints of 10-20-30-

40 yards. In-line skating. Run-jog-run laps.

Goalies: Increase standing flys to 4 sets. Add knee lifts (done on leg extension machine, tucking knee under the padded bar and lifting upward) 2 x 10.

In conclusion on this segment of off-ice drills, it may be suggested that we American coaches must be more imaginative in this area since we have less natural ice available to us than our Canadian counterparts. We can work off-ice for free whereas we must often pay for true ice. Hockey is expensive enough as it is; work your players off the ice in as many areas related to the game as possible. Save your precious ice-time for constant skating and movement. Or to put it another way, do the teaching outside and the drilling inside.

CONDITIONING FACTORS FOR ICE HOCKEY PLAYERS

— Recreational And More Competitive

— Preseason, In-Season And Off-Ice Work

The "recreational ice hockey player" skates once or twice per week, so the conditioning factor needed to compete in a game is often lacking.

Research shows that any person can reach 80% of their maximal conditioning level with just three aerobic workouts of 30-minutes duration per week. 80%! This translates to one hockey practice and two runs of 2-3 miles per week. If no hockey practice is available and the athlete only has games in which they must be in shape for, then three aerobic workouts to prepare for that game will be sufficient. Your options include any of these plans:

RUNNING: Three 2-mile runs per week. Try "run-jog-run" in which you intersperse 6-10 windsprints of 20-40 yards during the jog.

STATIONARY BIKE: Three 40-minute sessions per week (the caloric expenditure of 20 minutes on the bike roughly equates with a one-mile run). The stationary bike is more popular with professional hockey players and the legs are kept in shape, but the "wind" factor is a bit questionable.

The Philadelphia Flyers bicycle training program is as rigorous as it is excellent. Here it is:

Phase I:	4 min. at 70 rpm
	1 min. at 110 rpm
	repeat for 4 more sets
	total time: 20 min.

Phase II:	8 min. at 90 rpm
	45 sec. at 100 rpm
	90 sec at 70 rpm
	45 sec. at 100 rpm
	90 sec. at 70 rpm
	45 sec. at 100 rpm
	90 sec. at 70 rpm
	30 sec. at 100 rpm
	1 min. at 70 rpm
	30 sec. at 100 rpm
	1 min. at 70 rpm
	75 sec. at 100 rpm
	1 min. at 70 rpm
	30 sec. at 100 rpm
	1 min. at 70 rpm
	total time: 21 1/2 min.

ROWING MACHINES, STAIR CLIMBERS, AND SKI-TRACK MA-CHINES: Apply the same rule of thumb of three 30-minute sessions per week. In reality, the caloric expenditure may be greater than running for 30 minutes. With the stair climbers, however, some research has shown that knee problems can develop, so monitor this.

WEIGHTS: Unless there is minimal rest-time between sets (less than one minute), little or no aerobic improvement will be realized, although the general strength improvement is obvious.

IN-LINE SKATES: Apply the 30-minute, thrice-weekly rule since the aerobic benefits from skating are excellent and can roughly equate with running. (Subjective analyses suggest a ration of 2:3 in terms of running vs. skating; i.e., two minutes of running = three minutes of in-line skating.)

APPENDIX AND ACKNOWLEDGMENTS

PRACTICE PLAN

Date: **Time:**

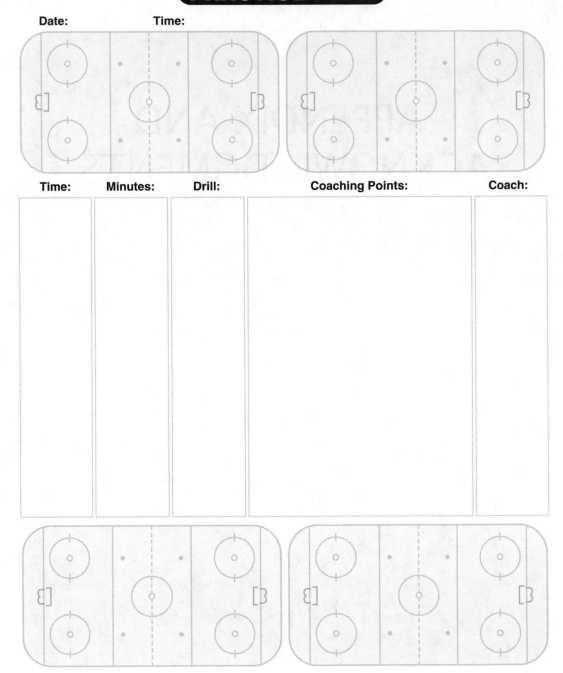

Time:	Minutes:	Drill:	Coaching Points:	Coach:

PRACTICE PLAN

Date: **Time:**

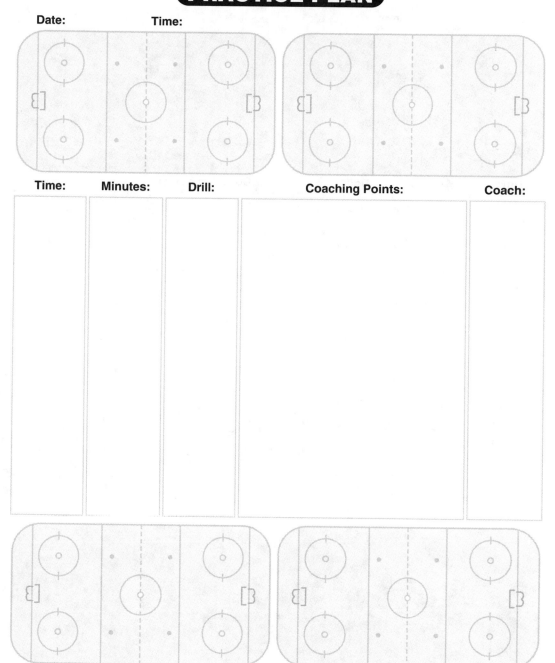

Time:	Minutes:	Drill:	Coaching Points:	Coach:

PRACTICE PLAN

Date:　　　　　　**Time:**

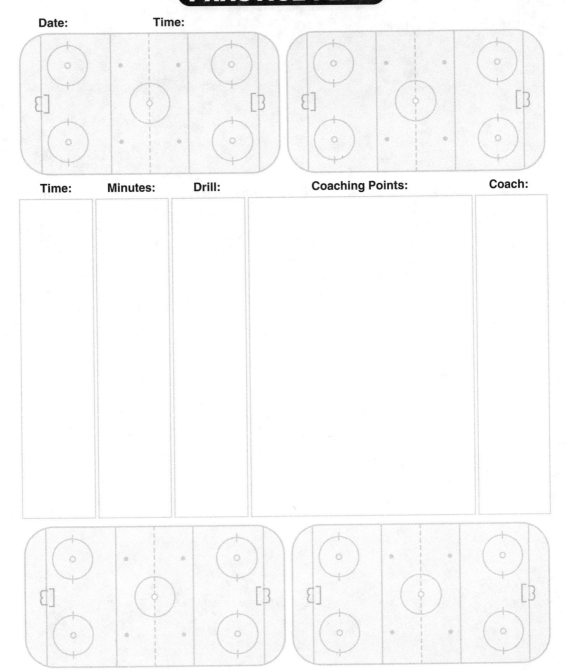

Time:	Minutes:	Drill:	Coaching Points:	Coach:

PRACTICE PLAN

Date:　　　　　　**Time:**

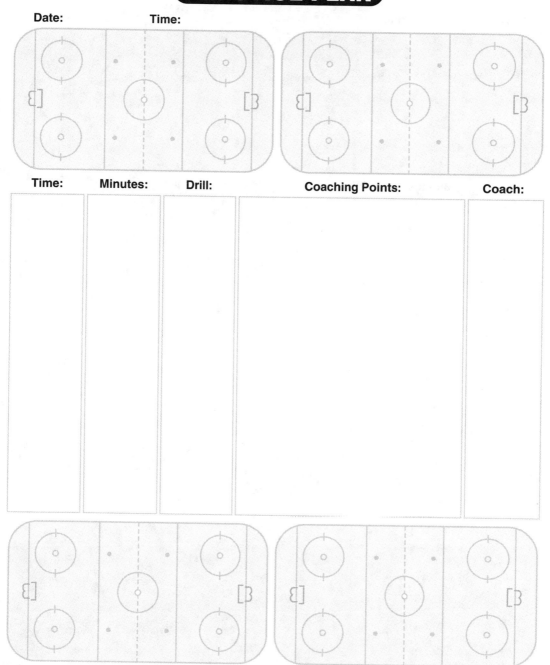

Time:	**Minutes:**	**Drill:**	**Coaching Points:**	**Coach:**

PRACTICE PLAN

Date: **Time:**

Time:	Minutes:	Drill:	Coaching Points:	Coach:

PRACTICE PLAN

Date: **Time:**

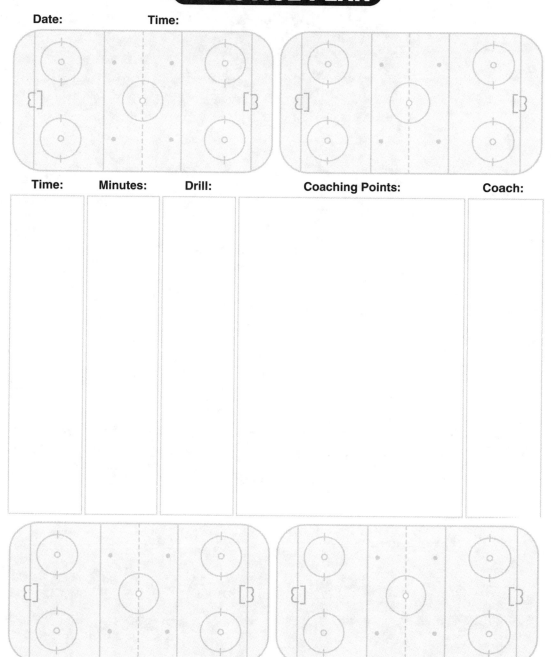

Time:	Minutes:	Drill:	Coaching Points:	Coach:

ACKNOWLEDGMENTS

I have worked with, and seen the work of, many fine ice hockey coaches over the years. This drill book has been a compilation of not only my efforts, but theirs, too. I would like to specifically recognize several people including Tim Zimmerman, Mike Reynolds, Pete Morris, Tim Taladay, Glenn Adamo, Rob Abel, Kevin Donald, Butch Porrino, Bob Blair, Lou Manzione, Vinny Claps, Rick Handchen, Pat Doyle, Bob Auriemma, Joe Patterson, Dick Trimble, Paul Cannata, Bob Cielo, and Derek LaLonde as well as my assistant coaches at Manasquan High School, Ken Biedzynski and Craig Beattie. Also to be cited are the coaching staffs at the many summer camps I have visited over the years including Princeton University, Providence College, Cornell University, the U.S. Military Academy at West Point, the Turcotte Stickhandling School, the Ocean Hockey School, Robby Glantz Powerskating clinics, and the Laura Stamm Powerskating programs.

Since coaching through drills is essentially a science of borrowing and modifying, all of the aforementioned have been of tremendous help in my endeavors. Each of the drills in this book was taught and tested by the author in various practices so that coaching points and warning signals could be included for the reader. Some drills were designed specifically for this volume, too.

It is hoped that each coach can find something that they would like to borrow and incorporate in their own practices.

Drill 'em and work 'em hard, but always with creativity, a purpose and a smile.

SUGGESTED READING LIST

Belmonte, Val. *USA Hockey Coaching Manuals*.

Belmonte, Val and Gary Gregus. *Half Ice Drill Book*.

Blatherwick, Jim. *Overspeed Training*.

Cielo, Bob. *Winning Hockey*.

Chambers, Dave. *The Incredible Hockey Drill Book*.

Lowdermilk, Dwayne. *How To Teach A to Z in Hockey*.

Pub-a-Practice. *Drill-It Hockey Practice Planner*.

Smith, Michael. *Hockey Drill Book*.

Smith, Ron. *Hockey Practice Drills*.

Stamm, Laura. *Powerskating*.

Wright, Gary. *Pass the Biscuit*.

Zulewski, Rich. *A Parents Guide to Coaching Ice Hockey*.